Starting An Archives

Elizabeth Yakel

Society of American Archivists
and
The Scarecrow Press
Metuchen, N.J. & London
1994

British Library Cataloguing-in-Publication data available

Library of Congress Cataloging-in-Publication Data

Yakel, Elizabeth.
    Starting an archives / by Elizabeth Yakel
       p. cm.
    Includes bibliographical references and index.
    ISBN 0-8108-2864-2 (alk. paper)
    1. Archives—Handbooks, manuals, etc. I. Title.
CD950.Y35   1994
025.17'14—dc20   94-14408

Contents

Acknowledgments

This volume owes many different things to many people. These acknowledgments give me a chance to say thank-you to some of the many hidden contributors to this manual. Readers at various stages of the development of this work, some anonymous, some not, made astute comments and suggestions. Jim O'Toole, SAA non-serial publications editor, was helpful and encouraging throughout the project. My friends and colleagues at the Maryknoll Mission Archives gave me insight into the practical questions and dilemmas faced when embarking on a new archival endeavor. A final proofreading by mother, the former editor, greatly improved the book. Any inaccuracies in this manual are mine alone.

I also want to thank the intrepid archivists who volunteered policies, forms, illustrations, and photographs for inclusion in the manual. To Elizabeth Adkins of the Kraft General Food, Nancy Bartlett of the Bentley Historical Library of the University of Michigan, Evelyn Cherpak of the Naval War Collection, Teresa Brinati of the Society of American Archivists, Todd Ellison of the Center of Southwest Studies at Fort Lewis College, Leonora Gidlund of the New York City Department of Records and Information Services, Mary Ellen Gleason, S.C., of the American Bible Society, Michael Grace, S.J., of Loyola University Chicago, Karen Jefferson and Donna Wells of the Moorland-Spingarn Research Center of Howard University, Mary Grace Krieger, M.M., of the Maryknoll Mission Archives, Elizabeth Nielsen of the Oregon State University, Bob Sink of the New York Public Library, Jac Treanor of the Archdiocese of Chicago, Tim Wilder of the Austin History Center, and Maureen O'Brien Will of the Evangelical Lutheran Church in America, I greatly value all of your submissions and trust.

Elizabeth Yakel
Ann Arbor, MI

Introduction: Three Archival Collections

Every institution is unique and so are its archival records. Still, vastly different organizations face similar problems regarding the best means of handling noncurrent records. What to save, where to keep materials of enduring value, and who should be in charge of the historical records are three of the questions which immediately come to mind. The following three case studies demonstrate the varied roads that institutions travel before facing these questions and the different conclusions that can be reached.

Eastern Urban Diocese

The Eastern Urban Diocese was established in the early nineteenth century and has grown steadily since that time. Located on the east coast, the diocese has been centered in an area of immigration and commerce since its inception. A prominent local archives contacted the diocese concerning the donation of its historical materials to the established repository. This prompted an investigation by several di-

Figure 1-1. Financial records, including journals and ledgers, in storage at Kraft General Foods Archives.

ocesan officials, a historian from a local university and an archivist. However, the bishop decided that an in-house archives was the best solution to establishing some organization over the collection and controlled access to the archives. This group, which evolved into the diocesan archives advisory board, realized the tremendous financial commitment it had assumed and wanted to phase the archives program into the diocesan budget over several years.

In the interim, local archivists banded together to write a grant to hire a full-time professional archivist, with the understanding that the diocese would fully support the archival program, including the professional and support staff after the grant ended. This model worked well. Within three years, the archivist and support staff were a vital part of the diocesan administration, had developed a series of workshops and lectures for the parishes, and opened materials to the public which were previously inaccessible for historical or genealogical research.

Midwestern Journey, Inc.

A large midwestern manufacturing firm, Western Journey, Inc., recently celebrated its centennial. Originally providing essential goods to homesteaders and settlers on their journey west, the company has expanded its product line throughout the twentieth century. In the basement of the original factory, renovated and refurbished more times than anyone can count, lie financial records spanning more than a hundred years. These ledgers document the initial bank loans which started the company, the role of the firm in the development and history of the municipality in which it is located, philanthropic grants to local organizations, and the donation of funds used for the expansion of the state university. One can also find outdated mail-order catalogs, advertising materials, and the original notebooks of the company's first engineers and product designers. The company has little daily need for these materials. The current advertising agency hired by the company, however, is interested in seeing the advertising materials that were used in the past. The state university archives has also

inquired about the existence of archival materials and the possible donation of the materials to that archives. Company officials never thought that any one would be interested in the "old stuff" in the basement, so their initial reaction to the request by the university archives was "great," but then they wondered just what was down there and decided that someone should have closer look before a final decision on the donation could be made.

The company called in an archival consultant. The consultant's final report provided a synopsis of the materials in the basement, discussed what the establishment of an archival program would entail in terms of institutional commitment of time, personnel, and money, and presented the pros and cons of donating the

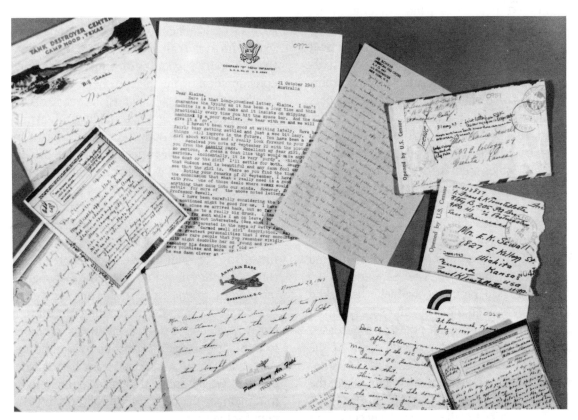

Figure 1-2. Types of paper records at the Oregon State University Archives.

records to the university archives. After careful consideration of all the issues with the aid of the consultant, the company's board of directors agreed to donate their noncurrent records and other materials to the university archives.

North Coast University

North Coast University is a large institution of higher education in the Pacific Northwest. Originally founded as an agricultural and normal school, the university now offers a full range of courses and has an enrollment of 25,000. Students attending the university have been active in social reform and antiwar movements, and the university library boasts a fine series of pamphlets and posters documenting both of these protest activities. The pamphlets are in the vertical files and the posters are in map drawers in the library. Both are readily accessible to students and can circulate. From time to time former graduates, university professors, and all the university presidents, some prominent and some not, have donated their papers, artifacts, and other materials related to their association with the college to the university. These have been duly given to the librarian who carefully stores them in locked "closets."

Although the librarian is unaware of it, there are many other such closets on the university campus. Generations of university newspaper editors have handed down the key to the closet of previous university publications and the photograph morgue. The secretaries in the anthropology department shudder when asked to retrieve something from the supply closet that houses the research notes of a deceased professor, offered to, but turned down by the family. Other noncurrent financial and corporate records are housed in the "vault" under the controller's office.

It is in this vault that the assistant controller

found himself one day looking for a deed to prove that the university owned a disputed parcel of land. Unable to find the necessary documentation, he accidentally overheard a lunch conversation concerning the wasted space in the library (e.g., the archival closets!). That afternoon he located the librarian in charge of the closet and searched the closets, still to no avail. However, in the papers of one of the former university presidents were the university trustees meeting from 1910. The trustees meeting minutes noted that the deed was to be registered by a certain member of the department of anthropology and returned to the President's office. As a last resort, the assistant controller telephoned the department of anthropology, learned of the anthropologist's notes, gained access to the notes, and found the missing deed, which had been registered with the county clerk.

The assistant controller's experience motivated him to start an advisory board to look into the university's records problem. After detailed consideration of the costs of beginning an archives were weighed against the cost of not establishing the program, a viable archival program was started. Today the archives is used by many administrative offices and several professors regularly plan assignments using the primary materials from the archives.

Just like the people in these stories, we all come into contact with potential archival materials everyday, perhaps without knowing it. In the office, we refer to an earlier report to corroborate policy decisions and settle disputes. In our studies, we may read notes from last year's seminar to assist in the preparation of a current paper. At home, we look at pictures of relatives to explain our ancestry to our own children. After using them, we may set these items aside, but they are all archival materials that help us to remember the past, live in the present, and plan for the future.

These documents, which we take for granted, are in danger of neglect and destruction. Individuals and organizations must take decisive action and direct responsibility for archival materials to ensure their preservation or these materials will be unavailable to future colleagues, historical researchers, and family members. Taking responsibility for archival materials means ensuring that they are preserved and made available in the best possible manner. This manual will provide guidance for individual organizations, institutions, and local community groups—that are investigating whether they should establish their own archival program—by briefly explaining the different elements necessary for an archival repository and by pointing out basic standards. *Starting an Archives* is designed to address the questions and concerns of administrators, resource allocators, and archivists in the initial stages of developing an archival program. Chapters 2 and 3 provide an overview of the major elements and commitment necessary to begin an archival program. Chapters 4 through 9 discuss initial policies, procedures, and standards necessary in an archival program.

MANUSCRIPTS: Although archivists often use the terms "archives" and "manuscripts" interchangeably, technically speaking, manuscripts are the papers of a person, an artificial collection of materials from a variety of places or persons, or individual items acquired because of some special significance.

2

Planning for Your Archival Program

In many cases the initiation of a records program comes during a major change, such as the death or retirement of a long-term employee, the celebration of an important anniversary, a major move, the restructuring of an organization or a change in a person's life. While it is a natural response to begin an archival program at these times, the historical records program cannot simply be viewed as a stop-gap measure to help ease a current "crisis." To ensure the continuous preservation of the unique materials, the archives must be strong enough to outlast the initial reason for its existence. The archival vision must be expanded. In short, the historical records program must demonstrate that it can be an integral part of the institution, is able to contribute to the overall mission of the institution, and that the archives are not just an executive broom closet.

In the beginning, the archivist must establish goals and objectives for the archival program which encompass all three definitions of the term "archives."

- Archives are the actual materials to be saved.
- The archives is the agency responsible for selecting the materials of enduring value.
- Finally, the archives is the place where historical records are preserved.

When used in this manual, the term "archival program" will signify all three definitions of archives under simultaneous development. Archival program will also encompass any organization which collects archival—strictly speaking—and/or manuscript materials.

Plans for the implementation of any archival records management or historical records program must address several important factors:

- The records to be collected,
- The administration of the agency,
- The physical site where the materials will be preserved, and
- The on-going support for the archives.

Establishing an archival program should not be done without careful consideration, ample planning, and well-defined goals. The initiation of an archival program entails a long-term and continuous commitment of an institution or organization to support, preserve, and make available a unique group of historical materials. An archival program requires a considerable investment of personnel and financial resources, even if its goals are relatively modest.

In the past, a general attitude existed among archivists and other institutional administrators that every organization should establish its own archival program. This attitude led to the initiation, as well as the failure, of many substandard archival programs without sufficient long-term institutional commitment. The archival records in these latter organizations have not been adequately preserved and their continued existence is doubtful. Today, this attitude is shifting. Archivists and administrators are focussing on the essential question of what is the best means of preserving records of enduring value. They are now asking and making tougher decisions concerning the best manner in which to preserve and make archival materials available.

Deciding not to establish an archival program can be more difficult than establishing and maintaining an inadequate archival program. Ceding the day-to-day management of the archives to a professionally run outside archival repository should not be viewed as giving away or losing one's history. Rather, it can be viewed as the most effective way to preserve and promote that heritage. This chapter will assist institutions and individuals in deciding if they should establish their own archival programs.

Prior to the establishment of an archival program, organizational administrators, with the advice of professional archivists and historians, should weigh the advantages and disadvantages of such a program. Important factors in the decision to initiate a historical records program are institutional commitment, sufficient resources, and an adequate facility. These factors should be constantly in mind during the primary stages of planning and development. They can be regarded as minimal standards and are grouped in the following three areas:

1. *Institutional Commitment*
2. *Archival Staff*
3. *Archival Facilities*

Institutional Commitment

The establishment of an archival program implies a long-term commitment on the part of an organization. This entails both a financial commitment and a willingness to give the archives the authority it needs to carry out its mission. Although the monetary implications of such an undertaking are often uppermost in an administrator's mind, it is essential that an archives (as agency) is given the authority it needs to operate. If an archives does not receive adequate authoritative support and power, it will never be able to fulfill its mission or become an integral part of the parent organization. Therefore, it will never be able to justify its budget or attain its goals.

It is essential that the archival records program be established with a strong administrative framework within an institution to ensure that it will become an integral part of the organization. The historical records program should be formally established by a written administrative order of the governing body. This directive should place the archives within the administrative structure so that the records program has the trust and confidence of the governing board. The archival program should have the authority to collect records from all parts of the organization and initiate access policies. The historical records program should also be recognized as an important and necessary participant in discussions of issues that relate to records and recordkeeping (such as computer applications and electronic mail) within the organization.

Finally, the archival program must be carefully placed in the organizational hierarchy to assure its independence as well as its ability to be successfully supported by higher, unquestioned authority, if the need arises. Administrators and archivists should not situate the archives within an administrative unit that has a different mission, even if that mission is related or periodically interdependent of that of the archives—for example, a public relations department. The archives can do much to assist a public relations department in developing brochures and advertisements or by researching the relationship of past events to current issues. Through outside researchers and outreach programs, the archives can do much to promote public relations. Yet, the goals and objectives of a historical records program are much broader. An institutional archives often does more internally within the organization to promote better recordkeeping practices and more systematic research on present questions of interest and importance to administrators within an organization.

Placement is also important because one office may not want to transfer records to the archives if the archives is administratively part of another office. Thus, the archives is more appropriately placed directly under a vice-president or general secretary in an organization where it has the authority to collect and manage its records independent of any given department. The other major area of institutional commitment to an archival program is its budget. This is a more readily visible, and not as subtle, area as that of administrative authority. The budget of an archival program can be divided into two areas :

Initiation and Capital Expenses

- Construction or renovation of the projected archival area. Few buildings contain areas ideally suited to housing and administering archival collections. This expense can include architects, structural engineers, renovation, shelving, etc., in the archival office, research, and storage areas. Proper design of these three areas can reduce future conservation costs and the chance of theft.
- Archival supplies. Beginning an archives, just like beginning an office, requires an extra purchase of basic supplies, including both archival and general office products.
- Equipment (e.g., computers, printers, microfilm readers). Computers and printers are a necessity in the management of the modern archives. With the computer, archivists can give users better service and can better retrieve, index, and describe archival materials

Ongoing Expenses

- Salaries and benefits for the archival staff. As in many offices, wages and benefits comprise the bulk of the archives' ongoing expenses.
- Archival and office supplies,
- Office maintenance (such as rent, telephone, postal and photocopying charges),
- Staff development (attendance at archival meetings, membership in archival organizations, purchasing archival publications). To provide the best service to the institution, archivists must keep abreast of developments in their profession such as advances in preservation techniques and dealing with new electronic media formats.

Because archival programs vary in size and have different responsibilities, goals, and objectives, and because the condition of the area to be renovated for the archives changes from one institution to the next, it is impossible to estimate expenses in this book. It should be noted, however, that although most archival programs are service-oriented and do not generate a significant income, the services that an archival program provides for an institution—in terms of research and reference assistance for other departments, educational programs, and records management—are worth a great deal to an organization, even though a monetary figure is (unfortunately) not often calculated for these activities.

Archival Staff

A professionally trained archival staff is essential for a successful archival program. It is sometimes confusing and difficult to evaluate archival skills, because there is no one correct method of entering the archival profession. As with the employment of any other professional, educational degrees or certification programs, attendance at advanced workshops, experience, and references must be checked against the requirements and skills needed for a particular archival position.

At this point, there is no graduate archival degree in the United States, though a graduate degree in archival science is offered in Canada. There are, however, a number of archival programs in the United States. Archivists are trained in American graduate schools, generally in the library and information science or history departments. The typical graduate training program for archivists in the United States includes specific courses in archival theory and administration. If an organization is starting an archives, the successful candidate for the position of director of the archives should possess at least 3-5 years of experience in the archival profession. This experience should be in a broad range of activities because the director will be responsible for either performing or overseeing all functions in the archives.

Many archivists have successfully entered the profession later in life. It is unfair to an archival program, an individual, and the institution as a whole, to place an individual in the archives assuming that it is a quiet resting place. The archives should be a place of activity and vitality and archivists do considerable physical tasks.

An archivist-candidate should have more than a vague interest in history. Having lived a long time and thus experienced more history is also not the most appropriate experiential qualification for an archivist. In addition to archival training, an archivist should have demonstrated administrative and management skills, knowledge of research techniques, reference practices, knowledge of research trends, a sensitivity to current historical issues as they relate to an archival program, and the initiative and insight to recognize and learn skills which are necessary for the development and success of the records program (whether these skills relate to computers or architectural renovation). While an institution can sometimes be successful in "picking someone out of the ranks" to train to become archivist, this is an extremely risky endeavor.

The archival profession and the skills needed to manage an archival program are rapidly changing, especially in the area of technology. Archival training is an ongoing process, even for those archivists with graduate level archival training. A single basic archival workshop does not "make" an archivist.

One institution may decide that it cannot afford to hire a professional archivist or that it can only afford minimal training for an internal candidate. Another institution may view itself as too small or too provincial to be concerned with technological developments. These institutions lack the vision necessary to establish a successful archival program. Without this vision and commitment, an organization probably cannot afford an archival program at all and should not consider initiating one.

Archival Facilities

The location and renovation of an archival facility is the third major area which should be discussed in the preestablishment phase of an archival program.

- Is there a suitable location within the building in which to administer and house historical materials?
- Can that area be renovated to accommodate the growth in the collection as well as to ensure the preservation of that collection for future generations?
- Is there sufficient space for the organization and use of archival materials?

Basic guidelines for the physical plant will be discussed in Chapter 9.

All of these basic guidelines may not be achievable in the first years of an archives existence, but the organization must actively work towards them. Goals and objectives are essential—as well as continual analysis of how well an archival program achieves the goals and objectives it has established for itself. If an organization finds that it cannot reach the attainable goals it has set for the archival program within the specified amount of time, the historical records program should cease to exist. At that point, other alternatives to preserve and make the records available should be explored. This experimental tactic should not be viewed as a waste of time and money, but rather as a means of saving on the slow, draining mainte-

DONATION means ceding all aspects of the administration and management of a group of archival materials to another institution. This includes the legal transfer of both physical property rights and literary copyrights to the material.

nance of a substandard archival program. Such an inferior effort creates an ongoing financial commitment that includes the too often uncalculated cost of volunteer labor, as well as the risk of losing valuable historical documentation.

There are many reputable archival repositories which will assume the responsibility for the archival records of another institution. If an organization finds that it is unable to support an archival program, locating one of these archival institutions is one means of preserving historical records. The archival materials can be donated outright, in which case both the legal property rights and the copyrights are transferred to the archival repository receiving the records. Another method is to deposit the records in an archival repository. In this case, the archival repository is a custodian of the records and administers the records according to prearranged policies.

Prior to any agreement between an organization and an archival repository, donors and depositors should carefully examine the ability

DEPOSIT is the placing of documents in the custody of an archival institution without transferring the legal title.

of the repository to organize, maintain, and provide access to their records. Organizations interested in donating—and particularly those interested in depositing their records in another archival repository—should be aware of the costs associated with the care and maintenance of archival records. A one-time or yearly donation may be in order, particularly if the records are on deposit and could therefore be removed at any time. For this reason. many archival repositories will not accept records on deposit. The administrators in institutions donating records should carefully consider the questions of access to the records and policies concerning the records. All restrictions and special instructions should be explicitly stated in writing as part of the deed of gift or certificate of deposit. A donating institution should always sign a deed of gift or a certificate of deposit which clearly states the responsibilities of both the donating institution and the archival repository receiving the materials.[2]

Role of Consultants

Archival consultants can be called in at any stage in the development or management of an archival program. However, they are often called in to assist in the initiation of an archival program. A consultant can be instrumental in establishing professional standards and developing a plan of action. A consultant should be used to help an organization review all aspects of the feasibility of starting an archival program.

Selecting an archival consultant can often be as difficult as hiring an archivist. Before choosing a consultant, his or her professional degrees and certificates, experience, and references should be checked. Archival students are sometimes required, as a part of their training, to examine existing archival programs or to do

feasibility studies for the establishment of archival programs in selected institutions. While the results of these papers are freely shared with the institutions concerned, few archival students have the experience or administrative skills necessary to offer authoritative advice on the major developmental issues involved, such as the feasibility of starting an archival program. Student papers can give an institution insight into the functions of an archival program, help an organization formulate essential questions to be addressed, and assist in the development of goals and objectives, but a consultant with more professional experience should be sought for advice and guidance on the initiation of an archival program.

The selection of a consultant is accompanied by the development of a detailed contract between the consultant and the institution. The organization should receive a written report from the consultant. The organization's expectations of the consultant should be clearly stated. Does the organization want basic policies drafted as part of the report? What kind of follow-up or ongoing relationship does the organization expect from the consultant?

The most productive consultant-organization relationships are those in which the organization actively works with the consultant toward the final report, policy development, etc. An organization that simply authorizes a consultative study on the feasibility of an archival program and then passively awaits the results will not gain as much because it will not have participated in the thought processes required for the establishment of an archival program, nor will it fully understand the archival concerns reflected in the final report. Also, the consultant will fail to gain as deep an insight into the organizational milieu and will not be able to develop a plan that best considers the overall mission, strengths, and weaknesses of the entire organization.

Archival Culture

Those who undertake archival programs should become immersed in related culture by visiting archival repositories, joining archival organizations, attending conferences, etc. It is essential that those individuals selected to assess the feasibility of beginning an archival program visit as many established programs as possible. Large and small operations, as well as different types of archives, should be viewed and analyzed. There is no better method of understanding the interrelationship of archival functions than to see the everyday activities of an archival program. Observers should note programmatic aspects to imitate, problems and pitfalls to avoid, innovative methods of dealing with constraints, and the possibilities of available through modern technology.

In general, archivists freely share policy documents and the history of their own archival programs. Establishing a relationship with archivists and archival repositories is important, and not just to answer archival reference questions. Relationships between repositories are essential to coordinate collecting policies, to share information on holdings, and to provide the best possible service to users in one's own institution. If an organization is establishing an archival program, care should be taken not to abuse the openness and goodwill of another archivist or archival repository or to use that individual or institution as a free consultant.

Many archival publications, conferences, and organizations are geared towards specific types of archives: businesses, historical societies, local governments, religious institutions, museums, hospitals, etc. While these may offer insight into specific local problems or organizational cultures, visiting a broad representation of archival institutions and reading a wide variety of archival literature aimed at different audiences will help an archivist to respond to a variety of daily archival concerns, as well as to potential problems and difficult situations. A good publication to begin learning about the nature of archives and the archivist's duties and responsibilities is James M. O'Toole's *Understanding Archives and Manuscripts,* the first volume of the Society of American Archivists' *Archival Fundamentals Series.*[3]

There are also many local, regional, and national archival organizations, some of which are listed in chapter 11 of this book. All of these organizations provide assistance in locating publications and educational opportunities. The Society of American Archivists can assist individuals in finding local archival networks.

After the group that studied the feasibility of instituting an archival program has reached its conclusion and has made a conscious, positive decision that the establishment of a new archival program is preferable, the governing body must affirm that decision. Only then should an institution move ahead with the actual establishment of an archival program. This decision can take time and may involve the effort of a diverse group of the institution's officials, archival consultants, or local archivists. However, once the decision has been ratified at the highest possible level, the initiation phase can begin in earnest.

3

Establishing an Archives

A historical records program serves many functions within an organization. First and foremost, it should further and assist in the overall purpose, mission, goals, and objectives of that institution. It does this by providing support services to other offices as well as by accomplishing specifically archival tasks.

Archival programs greatly vary in size, however all agencies which take care of historical records, from the National Archives and Records Administration (NARA) to the smallest local historical society, must embrace the same essential basic program elements. These elements are briefly introduced in the following paragraphs and are described in greater depth throughout this book.

Planning and Administration of the Archival Program

Archival administration encompasses the development of goals, plans, and priorities. It also deals with the initial formulation and periodic review of policies, budgeting, staff selection, supervision, and continuing education.

Collection Development

Collection development concerns the formulation and implementation of policies regarding the acquisition of materials and possibly the initiation of cooperative collecting with other organizations in a specific geographic area or with similar subject interests.

Appraisal

Appraisal is the process of analyzing the enduring historical, legal, administrative, or fiscal value of a group of records and their relationships with other groups of records. Not all records merit permanent retention in the archives.

Records Management

Records management is an implicit part of an archival program. It is essential for ensuring that today's records will be available in the archives of tomorrow. Many institutional archives provide some records management services for their organization. Archivists in organizations with records managers should be in constant contact with them to ensure that adequate documentation reaches the archives. Records management is not treated in depth in this manual, although archivists should be aware of the complementary responsibilities of archival and records management programs.

Arrangement

The arrangement of records is the activity most often identified with archives and archivists. Arrangement is the process of organizing archival materials in accordance with accepted archival principles to facilitate use. Some archivists and administrators erroneously assume that if there is someone organizing an institution's archival records, that therefore an organization has an archival program. Arrangement is only one function in a healthy archival program.

Description

Closely related to arrangement, but independent of it, is the process of describing archival materials. Although most archivists generally speak of "arrangement and description" in tandem, description requires an entirely different focus than arrangement. Description signifies the development of a written account (on paper or in a computer database) of the physical characteristics, content, and functional purpose of the records to further promote use. It is the final step in the process of establishing intellectual control over archival materials and provides the archivist and the researcher with some indication of what types of documents and subjects are covered in a collection and how the materials can best be used. The term "processing" is often used synonymously for the terms arrangement and description.

Reference

Use is the ultimate goal of all other archival functions. All other program elements should support and promote present and future usage of the collections. Reference encompasses a range of activities including developing policies for use, locating, analyzing, and providing information concerning records to in-house personnel or historical researchers.

Access

Access is one of the most difficult archival terms and one of the most delicate archival administrative problems. The term "access" is employed by archivists in two different senses, which can easily be confusing. First, access signifies the legal conditions by which archival materials are available for use. Second, access represents the actual ability to use the records as determined by their physical arrangement and any available description of the records. This book will discuss means of allowing legal, controlled access to materials and what considerations should be given to the development of access policies for different types of materials.

Outreach

Outreach encompasses promoting awareness of historical records, encouraging increased use of archival records, and identifying both new sources of archival records and potential new users of those materials. To do this, the archivist must develop activities which inform both personnel within an organization and outside researchers about the holdings of the archives, the value of specific materials for current issues or projects, and areas in the archives which are insufficiently documented. Archivists should view every contact with fellow employees, administrators, potential donors, and researchers as an opportunity for outreach and an occasion to inform people about the importance of archival materials.

Preservation: The Micro and Macro Environments

Preservation is the maintenance of archival materials in all formats to insure that they will be available for use by future generations. This activity should concentrate on everyday activities which can be done to extend the life of entire archival collections, not on heroic examples of restoration of single items.

The micro environment refers to the immediate environment in which archival materials are stored (e.g., boxes and file folders) and the different properties of various media of archival materials.

Basic knowledge of the physical plant—the macro environment—housing the archival records is essential for the effectiveness of all other functions, particularly administration and preservation planning. Repository management entails developing knowledge of the area in which the archival materials are housed and the administration of this physical plant to ensure that the records are preserved under the safest possible conditions and are used with care and prudence.

None of these archival functions can be dealt with individually. They are interdependent. The strength of an archival program depends on actions being taken in all these areas; monthly, weekly, and daily. Functions, such as arrangement and description, cannot be singled out, for any length of time, as being of the greatest importance. Other activities in the archives cannot halt for a year or two while all historical records are put in order. The strength and the survival of an archival program depends on establishing an inclusive ground plan that balances the competing needs of each of these activities. An archival vision, supported by realistic goals and objectives, is essential for the success of all archival programs.

Administration

All archival programs require several basic policy and authority documents to ensure their stability. These documents support and elucidate the administrative position, powers, and activities of the archives. They are the statement of authority, the mission statement, long- and short-term goals and objectives, the collection development policy, and the budget document which supports these initial four statements. These documents must be drafted prior to, or in the first stage of, the establishment of an archival program and should be approved by the highest authorities of the organization. After the working drafts are agreed upon, the feasibility of establishing an internal archival program can again be studied with the following questions in mind.

- What is the best location to carry out the goals of the archival program?
- Is the budget realistic for meeting those goals?

For a detailed look at archival administration, see *Managing Archival and Manuscript Repositories* by Thomas Wilsted and William Nolte, another volume of the Society of American Archivists *Archival Fundamental Series*.

Statement of Authority

A clear, concise statement of authority for the archival program is necessary to signify internal support and program scope. This statement should place the archival program within the established structure of an institution. The higher up in the organizational chart that the archival program is placed, the greater the chance of its success and of achieving its goals. This statement can be, but is not necessarily, part of the mission statement, which is described in the following paragraph.

Mission Statement

A mission statement further defines the vision for the archival program and its place within the larger institution.

Managing Archival and Manuscript Repositories states four basic questions which every mission statement should answer. These are

- What groups, activities, or experiences does the archives document?
- Why was the archival program initiated?
- What does the archives collect?
- What groups or interests does the archives serve?[4]

ARCHDIOCESE OF CHICAGO
5150 NORTHWEST HIGHWAY
CHICAGO, ILLINOIS 60630

Archives & Records Center
(312) 736-5150

Figure 4-1. Mission Statement for the Archives of the Archdiocese of Chicago.

Archives of the Archdiocese of Chicago

Mission Statement

The purpose of the Archives of the Archdiocese of Chicago is to collect, preserve, and make available for research the official records of the Archdiocese and those ancillary records which reflect the work of the Church within the Archdiocese. The Archives is erected in accordance with Canon 482, which charges the Chancellor with the responsibility for the Archives. The Assistant Chancellor for Archives & Records reports to the Chancellor and is granted canonical faculties to fulfill this mandate.

The Archdiocesan Archives seeks to promote an understanding of the origins, aims, and goals of the Archdiocese as reflected in the workings of the official Archdiocese agencies, institutions, and offices. Official archdiocesan records are defined as

> all recorded information, regardless of media type or characteristics, made or received and maintained by an agency, institution, or office in pursuance of its legal obligations or in the transaction of its business.

The Archdiocesan Archives also seeks to collect, preserve, and make available for research those records of individuals and organizations engaged in work which is reflective of the work of the Catholic Church in the Archdiocese. Such individuals and organizations may operate within the Archdiocese in an adversarial capacity, as a unit supervised by the Archdiocese, or as an advocate of the Archdiocese.

STATEMENT OF PURPOSE
OF THE
LOYOLA UNIVERSITY OF CHICAGO ARCHIVES

The Loyola University of Chicago Archives is charged with the responsibility of appraising, collecting, organizing, describing, preserving, and making available for research and reference use those official University records and those ancillary records of the University community of sufficient historical, legal, fiscal, and/or administrative value to warrant permanent preservation. "Official University records" include any and all documentation in any form produced or received by any employee of Loyola University of Chicago while engaged in the conduct of official University business. "University community" includes individual and collective members of the faculty, staff, administration, student body, and alumni of the University as well as any other individuals and organizations whose activities have relevance for the University.

The University Archives strives to provide adequate facilities for the retention and preservation of official university records. In addition, it facilitates efficient records management to further assure that permanently valuable records are preserved and to encourage efficient use of space within the University. In collecting these materials, the University Archives undertakes to recognize and honor matters of privilege and confidentiality.

The University Archives promotes knowledge and understanding of the origins, aims, programs, and goals of the University, and of the development of these aims, programs, and goals. It provides information services that will assist the operation of the University in addition to serving research and scholarship by making available and encouraging use of its collection by members of the University and the community at large. Furthermore, the University Archives serves as a resource and laboratory to stimulate and nourish creative teaching and learning.

The University Archives also appraises, collects, organizes, describes, preserves, and makes available for research and reference use records of individuals and organizations not directly connected with Loyola University of Chicago should the subject matter of the collection be particularly relevant to the collecting interests and strengths developed by the staff of the University Archives.

AMDG 9/90

Figure 4-2. Statement of purpose of the Loyola University of Chicago Archives.

KRAFT GENERAL FOODS ARCHIVES
MISSION STATEMENT

The mission of the KGF Archives is to act as the corporate memory for Kraft General Foods and support the company in its mission to be the leading food company in the world. The Archives plays a vital role in supporting current company operations, maintaining continuity and capitalizing on corporate heritage and brand equity.

Archives staff serves all company employees, with efforts targeted to brand management, legal/trademark, corporate affairs, consumer affairs, marketing services, human resources and sales. We also serve individuals outside the company who have an interest in KGF's history, including consumers, scholars of the food industry, collectors of KGF memorabilia and the media.

We will accomplish our mission by acquiring, preserving and providing information from materials documenting the history of the company and its products, predecessor companies, employees, plants and policies.

Pursuit of this mission provides KGF with the strategic competitive advantage that is inherent in its rich historical legacy.

Figure 4-3. Mission Statement for the Kraft General Foods Archives.

MISSION STATEMENT : a succinct enunciation of the purpose of an archival program and how it relates to its larger constituency or organization.

Planning and Setting Priorities

Archival programs—new and old—require a planning document that states long- and short-term goals. In an institutional archives, the plan should consider the mission of the archives as well as the purpose and immediate goals of the parent organization. The plan should be developed by the archives staff and approved by the parent organization. Initially, every archival program should develop an operating plan for the first two years as well as an outline of projected activities for the first five years. Goals should be drafted in all the areas of archival administration listed in the previous chapter.

Each goal statement is developed in several steps. First a broad goal is identified and articulated. This goal may take years to achieve or it may be an on-going issue of importance for

---

EXAMPLE

Outreach

Goal: Increase use of the archives.
Objective: Increase the awareness of archives resources by a specific user group (e.g., local college history departments)
Activities:
1. Send an invitation to visit the archives with brochures to all local history department heads.
 2. Arrange follow-up calls and appointments to discuss specific means of using the archives in the college's history curriculum.
Materials Needed: Brochures
Person Responsible: Archivist
To Be Completed By: June 1

---

the archival program. Second, objectives or less broadly defined goals should be formulated. One goal may require several objectives in order to be fulfilled. Third, specific activities are designed to reach each objective. Activities should be eminently doable within a reasonable amount of time. If an activity can not be accomplished in a timely fashion, it is probably too ambitious and should be broken down into several smaller activities. Fourth, the person responsible, the materials necessary to complete the activity, and a target completion date should be established. Breaking each goal down into achievable activities is essential in the formulation of realistic plans.

Once a plan has been formulated, the goals and objectives should be ranked by priority. In ranking goals, the archivist should consider both the particular needs of the archives as well as the broader concerns and goals of the parent organization. If the archivist is working on a five-year plan, activities can build upon each other throughout that period to achieve larger goals.

Self-evaluation and Program Assessment

The archives staff should periodically step back and review their progress and achievement in terms of their mission statement and the plan which they have established for themselves. The period of programmatic review and self-evaluation is a time to reaffirm mission, goals, priorities, and policies. It is also an opportunity for the staff to confirm commitment to the ideas represented in these documents, as well as to revise plans in light of new developments. There are three recently published tools to assist archivists in the evaluation and planning processes. Paul McCarthy's *Archives As-*

[Title Page]

LOYOLA UNIVERSITY OF CHICAGO ARCHIVES

ANNUAL REPORT

JULY 1, 1991 — JUNE 30, 1992

TABLE OF CONTENTS

[Table of Contents]

Figure 4-4. A sample Annual Report—Loyola University of Chicago Archives.

sessment and Planning Workbook leads an archival program step by step through the assessment and planning processes towards the formation of a realistic plan.[5] This workbook treats all archival functions and includes a checklist of possible activities related to improving each one. *Strengthening New York's Historical Records Programs* assists archival programs in the task of self-evaluation and has clearly defined minimal standards for archives to follow.[6] The *Guide and Resources for Archival Strategic Preservation Planning* (GRASP) combines three different program evaluation tools that examine an archives preservation problems.[7] The first section is a computer-assisted survey to determine a repository's preservation needs, the second part gives an institution specific strategies to follow for better preservation planning, and the third section lists resources for preservation planning—from printed materials to vendors to assist in averting disaster or helping should one occur.

An annual report will help by providing a review mechanism at a higher level. In addition to informing members of some of the institution's information base and heritage, the annual report provides the archivist with an opportunity to examine the past accomplishments, the present state, and the future direction of the archives. Through this document, the archivist can better evaluate progress toward objectives and gauge the effectiveness of all archival activities. More broad-based knowledge of archival activities increases support. The archival program is strengthened when there is widespread involvement in, and understanding of, the archives.

Position Descriptions

All staff members in an archival or historical records program should have position descriptions. This includes all paid, volunteer, full, and part-time employees. Position descriptions are an important tool to assist members of the archival staff to define their duties and reflect on their activities. It helps others in an institution or a community to see the varied responsibilities and diverse activities expected from the archives staff.

Budget

A budget is necessary for any entity to function properly and the archivist should maintain good financial records of expenses. The budgetary process in many institutions provides another opportunity, along with the annual report, to educate supervisors and co-workers about the potential of an archival program. Arguing for expenses can also assist the archivist in formulating priorities and more clearly articulate how individual archival activities fit into the overall goals of the archives and the parent institution.

Advisory Boards

An advisory board is composed of archivists in one's area with years of experience and knowledge of a community, as well as established members of the local community or the parent institution. Ideally, board members should all be interested in the archival program, be invested in its survival, and not have any competing interests. An advisory board should bring both archival expertise and political knowledge of the parent institution to the archival program. Having administrators from the parent institution on the board is a means of enlisting their support and disseminating information concerning the archival program within the organization. To avoid any future problems, it is advisable for board members to have rotating terms.

Collection Development, Appraisal, and the Initial Stages of Archival Control

This chapter continues the process of starting an archives by discussing the drafting of another major policy statement. The collection development statement defines area(s)—subject, geographical, etc.—of documentation that the repository will collect. Implicit in the collection development policy is the need to select materials. The selection process is necessary to provide sufficient documentation of all areas targeted by the collection development policy. This chapter also demonstrates how the archives can collect basic information on groups of records and establish physical control over large amounts of materials that can be refined later in the appraisal, arrangement, and description processes. More detailed information concerning collection development, appraisal, and the life cycle of records is available in *Selecting and Appraising Archives and Manuscripts* by F. Gerald Ham.[8]

Collection Development

Strong archival programs not only have a firmly established administrative base and institutional support, but also maintain a clear vision of the intended growth of the archival collection. This vision is articulated in a collection development or acquisitions policy, which grows from the statement of authority and the mission statement.

Archivists and records managers recognize that records have a natural life cycle. Offices create records in the natural course of their business and use these records for a certain period. After this time has elapsed, the office staff's administrative usage of the documents declines. At that point, materials can be transferred to the archives. Some documents retain their evidential, e.g., legal or financial, value even after their daily administrative use is over. Some materials document a certain philosophy or activity which occurred at a specific point in time and thus acquire a historical value in the archives. When transferred to the archives, these documents may be of only occasional use to the initial creator or compiler, but they take on a new life and become important to other users for reasons entirely different from their original purpose. Archivists and records managers can assist offices in the process of life cycle through the formulation of collection development priorities and by the establishment of specific timetables and procedures (e.g., records schedules) for more current records to be transferred to the archives/records center or destroyed.

In planning for collection development, the archivist should also consider whether there are any other similar collections in other offices, the geographic area, or perhaps even the country. There are enough archival materials available that historical records repositories should cooperate, rather than compete. If an institution is considering beginning a new collection or expanding into a new collecting area, regional—and in some cases archives across the United States—should be contacted to ensure that there is really a need for a new collection.

The collection development policy should take a broad view of potential archival sources and the formats of material to be collected. Materials destined for the archives are in a variety of different media: paper, audio or video tapes, computer disks, photographs, film, artifactual objects, and art works. Although arguments can be made for the archivist not assuming responsibility for artifactual objects and works of art, if there is no one else in the organization to care for these alternative formats, the archivist, as custodian of the organizational culture, may choose to assume the responsibility.

Table 5-1. Elements to Consider in Developing a Collection Policy

I. Statement of Purpose (abbreviated from Mission Statement)
II. An indication of user community (the variety of persons / programs supported by the collection)
    A. Topics of Research (internal and external)
    B. Exhibits
    C. Outreach
    D. Publications (internal and external)
    E. Other
III. Clientele served by the collection
    A. Internal Offices
    B. Researchers (Professors, Students, etc.)
    C. General Public
    D. Other
IV. Priorities and limitations of the collection
    A. Present identified strengths
    B. Present collecting level
    C. Present identified weaknesses
    D. Desired level of collecting to meet all program goals
    E. Geographical, chronological, topical areas collected
V. Cooperative agreements with other archival repositories regarding collecting or documentation strategies
VI. Statements concerning resource sharing
VII. Summary of the deaccessioning policy
VIII. Procedures or policies affecting the collecting policy
IX. Procedures for monitoring the progress and reviewing the collection development policy guidelines

Adapted from Faye Phillips, "Developing Collecting Policies for Manuscript Collections," American Archivist, Winter 1984.

The COLLECTION DEVELOPMENT or ACQUISITION policy sets directions for future archival accessions and addresses known gaps in the existing collection.

AUSTIN HISTORY CENTER
COLLECTION DEVELOPMENT POLICY

The Austin History Center is a research institution for local history. Its mission is to collect and preserve current and historical materials about Austin and Travis County in order to make them readily available to researchers.

Scope of Materials

As a research center, the Austin History Center (AHC) places primary emphasis on the informational value of the materials collected, which include:

  a. publications issued by the City of Austin, Travis County, or their departments. AHC serves as the official depository for municipal documents published by the City of Austin and as the state's depository for Travis County records in the County Records Project.
  b. materials containing information about some aspect of Austin and Travis County (A/TC), including its residents, geography, economics, government, natural and built environment, businesses, institutions, and organizations.
  c. some items relating to Texas history. These are included as background sources, or because they contain significant information about A/TC or their residents, or because they illuminate Austin events, but the collection is in no sense a Texas collection.

Because aesthetic and historical value alone are of secondary importance in meeting informational needs, and due to considerations of space and conservation, artifacts are not sought for the collection.

Clientele

As a section of the Austin Public Library, the AHC has as its primary mission the provision of information to the citizens of Austin. This means that our purpose in preserving the unique source materials is to make them available to all citizens, not just scholars. Among the primary user groups of the collection are city staff, students and faculty members, business persons, historic preservationists, genealogists, journalists, and other interested citizens.

These users seek current and historical information about local events, businesses, and organizations, neighborhoods and community leaders, the built environment, city services and publications, demographics and other statistical data.

Collection Units

The AHC collection is composed of many individual collections, which are:

  a. Architectural Archives   f. House/Building File (HB)
  b. Archives   g. Map Collection
  c. Austin File (AF)   h. Periodicals
  d. Biography File   i. Photography Collection
  e. General Collection   j. Recordings

Figure 5-1. First page of a collection development policy from the Austin History Center, Austin Public Library. Many of the topics are treated in greater depth later in the policy.

Ongoing Tracking of Records in the Archives: Surveys

To assess how the actual archival collection relates to the collection development policy and what priorities and goals should be established in the area of collection development, it is essential that the archivist have a good sense of the quality of documentation in the archives and in the institution as a whole. To acquire this information, the archivist must develop a thorough understanding of the functions and responsibilities of all parts of the organization, including record creating and recordkeeping practices. Knowledge of record creating and recordkeeping practices is gained through records surveys within the archives and throughout the organization or community as a whole.

When an organization formally establishes an archival program, a group of materials already designated as "archival" is often stored away awaiting attention. A first step for the archivist is to inventory these holdings. This inventory or survey is intended solely as a broad overview of the existing archival materials and should not include detailed descriptive information. A standardized form should be developed on which to note the following general information concerning these materials:

- office of origin/creator/compiler,
- the inclusive dates,
- measurement (in standard linear or cubic feet),
- present location, and,
- if feasible within the boundaries of an initial inventory, brief organizational, content, and preservation notes.

Even if the archival program does not have access to a computer, the collection of standardized basic information for all archival materials during the accessioning, arrangement, and descriptive processes is important since it can later be input easily into a computer system.

After basic information has been gathered from records existing in the archives at the beginning of the archival program, a records survey should also be carried out in the offices of the organization as a whole, either simultaneously with, or immediately after, the "archival" inventory. Data, as described above, should be systematically collected in all offices and agencies over which the archives has authority.

Within an organization as a whole, a records survey can either be carried out by the archival staff, or by employees in each office. The decision concerning who should carry out the records survey in offices is often difficult to make, but the pros and cons of different means should be taken into consideration. There will be greater consistency in the data and fewer questions concerning the information collected if the archival staff carries out the entire survey. Office directors will also view the importance of the survey differently and require various degrees of attention and accuracy. If detailed instructions, a clearly stated data collection process, and some staff training are not developed to introduce the office survey, the archives staff may spend large amounts of time answering questions, even if they are not completing the actual survey. However, the physical logistics

---

Cubic feet = width x length x depth (measured in inches) divided by 1728. This means that standard archival shelving measuring 42 inches in length, 18 inches in width, and with shelves staggered at 12 inch intervals filled with archival materials would equal 4 linear feet or approximately 6.3 cubic feet.

---

of some corporations and organizations will necessitate multiple surveyors who have never before thought of their records as archival. The survey process is time consuming, particularly since it should be accomplished while balancing and not neglecting all other archival functions.

A records survey can also be done in the context of a local community, state, or nationwide search for archival materials concerning specific subjects. This survey can be done either to locate existing complimentary collections to which researchers can be referred or to search for potential new collections. In the latter case, this is often referred to as "field work." Archivists involved in field work contact potential donors (e.g., former company presidents and officials) whose records would contribute to the overall collecting policy and scope of the archival repository and solicit materials. Archival programs should be careful not to misrepresent the archives and to make sure that they can ethically care for, maintain, and make available over the long term any collections which they solicit. The Society of American Archivists "Donor's Guide" and the 1992 "Code of Ethics"9 indicate a number of important guarantees which should be provided by any archives that encourages outside donation.

When the results of the archival inventory and records survey have been collected, they must be analyzed. The archival staff should look at two primary aspects of the data collected concerning the records.

1. The quality of documentation or how well the materials document processes, departments, and activities.
2. The quantity of documentation or the amount of materials.

The quality of documentation affects collection development concerns and policies.

FIELD WORK involves the identification of potential collections for transfer to the archives, contacting the potential donors, and ensuring that the archives gains legal control over the materials if they are given to the archives.

There are two aspects to the quality of documentation. First, there is the quality of the information itself or the informational value. The informational value concerns the scope and reliability of the data in the records. Second, the quality of records is judged by their evidential value. Records contain evidential value of organizational activities, processes, functions, decisions, etc., which provide information on records creation, the records creators, and the recordkeeping processes. Knowledge of these records creators, records creation, and recordkeeping processes is essential for an identifying of the context in which the records were created. Understanding the context is essential for effective administrative reuse or historical use of the records.

In some institutions, the archives also possesses the responsibility for more current records management. These initial records surveys are also vital in establishing a records management program. If done well, these surveys can be used to schedule the future transfer of records currently held in administrative offices to the archives. The surveys also provide essential information on recordkeeping practices and database management, which will effect records throughout their life-cycle. The records surveys also act as an appraisal tool to assist the archivist in determining which records have permanent value and which materials can be scheduled for disposition after a certain number of years.

If there is a records manager already working in an organization, the archivist can benefit from the records manager's surveys. The archivist should study these carefully and note which materials should be transferred to the archives for permanent retention. The archivist should be aware that the records manager is primarily concerned with legal, fiscal, and administrative values of records. Once these values have passed, particularly the legal requirements of record retention, the records manager will follow the established schedule for records destruction. It is the responsibility of the archivist to note the possibility of continuing administrative, historical, or artifactual value.

Appraisal

The collection development policy is implemented through the process of appraisal. Appraisal is the process of determining the value and thus the disposition of records based on their current administrative, legal, and fiscal uses; their potential evidential, informational, and intrinsic value; their relationship to other records; and their condition. For archivists, value is usually not considered in monetary terms. Archivists weigh the different types of values of records in deciding which records to keep, how long they should be kept, and in what format the information should be retained.

Administrative, legal, and fiscal values demonstrate an ongoing need by an individual or company to retain certain documentation for the current or future conduct of business. As stated earlier, evidential value is the ability of a group of records to illustrate the nature and work of their creator or the functions and activities of the larger institution. Archivists assess the informational value of records by projecting the possible uses of the records for reference and research determined by the information they contain on persons, places, and events.

APPRAISAL is the process by which archivists evaluate records. It is through this process that selected records are determined to be of enduring value.

Intrinsic value is the inherent worth of a document based on an analysis of its age, content, usage, media, and circumstances of creation. These factors, among others, should all be considered at some point in the appraisal process.

Appraisal can be done at the item, file, or series level, depending on the type of records being appraised and on institutional priorities and policies. Appraisal takes place at different intervals during the process of identifying materials for placement in the archives.

Before the records even reach the archives, during the initial office survey or regular field work, records may be shown to the archivist which contain no enduring value. Later, during accessioning, the archivist has another opportunity to review of the records. During accessioning, obvious duplicates and other materials of no value are often discarded. Most records, however, require more time-consuming and careful evaluation at a later date. Collections which have been part of an archives for many years may also be reappraised in light of further information and examination and then deaccessioned. In no case should appraisal be left solely to the discretion of other administrators. Appraisal is one of the archivist's most basic and important responsibilities. It can be aided by administrators or legal counsel, but should never be determined solely by them.

Records should not be destroyed without ample consideration and examination. Archivists and other administrators should also avoid attempting to solve other, separate dilemmas, such as access to confidential materials or preservation problems (mold, infestation) through the appraisal process. Sensitive materials, which often contain personal details, can in many instances be made available after a set period of time has passed, thus protecting individual privacy. In this way, future historians are provided with unique insights into the lives and thoughts of individuals unavailable from other sources and have the opportunity to write more informed historical studies. Confidential materials, such as case files, can also be valuable for statistical research or studies which do not identify specific individuals. Materials deemed too sensitive for research today or which do not present the organization in the best possible manner should not be destroyed simply because they pose an access problem. Also, materials requiring extensive conservation treatments should not be discarded automatically. Although tempting at times, getting rid of one's sticky, expensive, and time-consuming access and preservation problems during appraisal distorts factual evidence for future generations and does future researchers a great injustice.

Ongoing Tracking of Records in the Archives: Accessioning

Archival materials should be tracked from the moment they enter the archives by establishing basic intellectual and physical control over the records. In this way the archives staff can immediately assess what has been done and what needs to be done to make a collection ready for research use.

Along with establishing intellectual control and physical control over a group of materials, the archivist must secure legal custody of the records. For an institutional archives, the statement of authority and mission statement should clearly indicate that the organization's

Figure 5-2. Staff member of the Austin Public Library working with archival materials in the Austin History Center.

own archives is the sole, official repository of the institution and that any materials created or compiled in the course of business are the property of the organization. Therefore, materials received from departments within an organization can simply be accompanied by a brief transfer/inventory form when they are sent to the archives. This transfer/inventory form should be signed by the department head and acknowledged by the archivist. It can be completed by either departmental or archival personnel, depending on the organization. This

INTELLECTUAL CONTROL is gaining a degree of mastery over the scope or content of records. This is done through analysis of the records and by learning about the agency or person through outside sources.

Figure 5-3. Records being transferred from a University of Michigan office to the Bentley Historical Library.

form contains the same elements noted in the inventory form shown on page 36 and will contain a list of all file folders. Descriptive notes should indicate the existence of confidential materials and the availability of the records for research.

Outside materials donated to the archives must be accompanied by a "Deed of Gift" (see Appendix A), which cedes all property rights and any copyrights held by the donor. Ideally,

---

PHYSICAL CONTROL is establishing command over aspects of the collection such as quantity and location.

---

the deed of gift should give the archives the right to do whatever it deems professionally responsible regarding the collection. The deed of gift also states the precise terms of access to a collection as agreed upon by the archives and the donor and may give donors a chance to ask for return of any materials which the archives plans to discard if the donation of the original records was not taken as a tax deduction.

The deed of gift is a legal document and as such is affected by state and federal tax laws. This is particularly true if the donors wish to take a tax deduction for records that they donate to the archives. Every deed of gift must be individually crafted to a certain extent to reflect the terms of a specific donation and the pertinent state and federal laws. Therefore, the "model" deed of gift agreement is only a model and cannot simply be adopted without changes. As with all legal documents, the organization's attorney should review it prior to its use by archives personnel. We live in a litigious society and elaborate, complex deeds of gift are a reality to protect archival institutions and donors. A deed of gift may also specify that the archives will organize the materials within a given amount of time, care for the collection in a manner to ensure its preservation, and make the collection available for research. An archivist cannot appraise archival materials for tax purposes if those records are destined for the archives for which he or she is responsible.

Copyright law is difficult and sometimes confusing to understand. A donor may own a collection physically, but may not own the copyright to all materials in the collection. For example, a former company president donates her personal papers to your archives. The collection consists of her own correspondence and that of friends, family, and colleagues. She owns only the copyright to her letters, stories, etc., which she wrote and therefore she is only able to cede copyrights to these materials to the archives. Copyright in the other materials is still held by those individuals who created them. The same is true of incoming correspondence in an institutional archives.

Along with establishing a strong administrative base, gaining both physical and intellec-

ACCESSIONING is the process of accepting custody of archival materials and recording that activity. DEACCESSIONING is the process of removing materials from the archives either to give to another, more appropriate archival program or to destroy the information.

tual control over the collection should be an archives top priority. The initial inventory of materials completed by the archivist upon the establishment of the archives serves as a means of retroactively accessioning materials. As the archives begins actively to collect records, new archival materials should be accessioned immediately upon entry into the archives. The records transfer form serves as part of the accession record. Accessioning establishes immediate physical control over all materials, some intellectual control (brief contents notes can be noted on the accession form), and provides important preservation information, such as whether the records have been damaged by water or insects. After the archivist receives records with a completed transfer form from another internal department or a deed of gift, they should be formally accessioned. Acces-

Figure 5-4. Formal donation of archival materials by the Daughters of Isis to the Moorland-Spingarn Research Center, Howard University.

```
                    MARYKNOLL MISSION ARCHIVES
                    RECORDS TRANSMITTAL FORM

┌─────────────────────────────────────┬───────────────────────────┐
│ Maryknoll Fathers and Brothers       │ Date:                     │
├─────────────────────────────────────┼───────────────────────────┤
│ Maryknoll Sisters Congregation       │ Contact Person:           │
└─────────────────────────────────────┴───────────────────────────┘

┌─────────────────────────────────────────────────────────────────┐
│ Name of Transmitting Office/Region:                               │
│                                                                   │
└─────────────────────────────────────────────────────────────────┘

                                          For Office Use Only

┌─────────────────────────────────┐
│ Type of Transfer:               │
│ Office Records                  │
│ Personal Papers     ____        │
│ Regional Records    ____        │
│ Media               ____        │
│ Photographs         ____        │
│ Artifacts           ____        │
└─────────────────────────────────┘

┌─────────────────────────────────────────────────────────────────┐
│ Description of Contents:                                          │
│                                                                   │
│                                                                   │
│                                                                   │
│                                                                   │
└─────────────────────────────────────────────────────────────────┘

┌─────────────────────────────────────────────────────────────────┐
│ Estimated Volume:                                                 │
│ #Linear Feet                        #Boxes    ____                │
│ #File Folders    ____               Other     ____                │
└─────────────────────────────────────────────────────────────────┘

┌─────────────────────────────────┬───────────────────────────────┐
│ Restrictions:                    │ Shelving Location:            │
└─────────────────────────────────┴───────────────────────────────┘

┌─────────────────────────────────────────────────────────────────┐
│ Legal Custody:                                                    │
└─────────────────────────────────────────────────────────────────┘

┌─────────────────────────────────────┬───────────────────────────┐
│ Received by:                         │ Date:                     │
└─────────────────────────────────────┴───────────────────────────┘
```

Figure 5-5. A sample Records Transmittal Form from the Maryknoll Mission Archives.

sion files can be set up in a number of ways. They can be chronological or alphabetical according to the name of the departments and individual donors or they can be classified in a system where each department or office is represented by a unique number. Chronological accession files are often assigned numbers according to the year (eg., 1992-1, 1992-2, etc. signifying the first, second, etc. accessions during 1992). In this way it is easy to determine how much archival material entered the archives during a given year, information that is essential for archival management. Alphabetical accession files should be cross-referenced so that the archives can calculate the amount of materials which entered that archives during a given year. Chronological accession files should be cross-referenced by department or donor. A classified system would be appropriate for an archives with many records transfers. It would identify the year of the donation, the donor office, and the donation number (first, second, third, etc.) for the year (e.g., 1994-16-2).

During accessioning the archivist should set priorities and establish the order by which materials will be treated. Furthermore, the archivist should determine the depth of treatment in terms the appropriate amount of time which should be spent on the archival arrangement and descriptive functions outlined in the next chapter.

Increasing Control over Archival Records: Arrangement and Description

The Process of Arrangement and Description

The most striking difference between archival records and library materials is how they are organized. The most decisive factor in the organization of archival materials is their *"provenance"* or origin. Books are created to provide information on a specific topic and are physically organized by subject. By their nature, archival records are an organic byproduct of an institution, activity, or person. Therefore, maintaining the context in which archival materials were created is absolutely essential to future historical understanding of an organization, individual, or activity. Archivists have found that the best method of maintaining the context is to organize records according to their "provenance" or creator. Fredric M. Miller's *Arranging and Describing Archives and Manuscripts* treats the principles and practicalities of archival arrangement and description in greater depth. [10]

The importance of provenance is illustrated in the following example. A corporate archives may receive records from its board of directors regarding the closing of a factory. Also, once the factory has closed, the records of that factory may be transferred to the central corporate archives. Both sets of records concern the closing of the factory, but they should not be inter-

---

PROVENANCE has been adopted from the French language. In archival parlance it means that materials from one records creator/compiler should not be intermixed with those of another records creator/compiler despite similarities in subject matter.

Figure 6-1. A staff member at the Archives of the Evangelical Lutheran Church in America accessioning archival materials.

filed. The perspective held by the board of directors on the closing may be radically different from the view provided by the factory's own records. By preserving both the records of the board and the factory, the archivist will be able to document the different functions and actions of the factory and the board during the closing and be able to maintain the integrity of the differing administrative and historical perspectives represented in the two sets of records. Intermingling records from these different origins would distort the historical record by muting the voices in the records, and making them largely indistinguishable. Once destroyed, provenance is almost impossible to restore.

Each group of archival records is composed of different levels of materials. In the corporate records cited above, each office or department maintains its own set of records. When transferred to the archives, the records from each office can be considered a record group, or a body of organizationally related materials created or compiled by the same entity or person. Within the records from each office, such as the personnel office, there are many record series or simply "series," e.g., a group of related files maintained as a unit by the creator or compiler. For example, the personnel office may send the following record series to the archives.

- Former Employees' Personnel Records
- Case files of settled legal disputes regarding the Personnel Department
- Files related to reducing cost of Employees Health Care
- Employee Policy Guidelines / Manuals (outdated versions)

A series is usually composed of individual file units or other similar types of material (e.g., account books, reels of magnetic tape), organized in a more or less discernable order. A similar type of material does not only signify physical type, but also having a similar administrative or informational characteristics. For example, the series of Former Employees Personnel Records, may be organized alphabetically by last name or by year of termination. The order in which the archives receives materials is referred to as the "original order." The original order should only be disrupted if it seriously

A "RECORD GROUP" is a body of organizationally related materials established on the basis of provenance. A "RECORD SERIES" or "series" is a group of materials which are organized or maintained by a records creator/compiler as a unit because of similar subject content, origin, or ease of use.

Figure 6-2. Videotapes and files in storage at the Kraft General Foods Archives. Note that the record group, subgroup, and series are clearly identified.

impedes research and retrieval. After the record group and the series, the next elements of the archival hierarchy are the file units and the individual item.

Five Levels of Arrangement (derived from Oliver Wendell Holmes)[11]

- **Repository**
- **Record Group / Collection**
- **Series (Subseries)**
- **File Unit (Folder, Volume, Reel of Magnetic Tape or Film, etc.)**
- **Item**

Before any archival collections are processed, each should be ranked by the amount and depth of archival treatment, based on cur-

ARRANGEMENT is the intellectual and physical organization of records with regard to archival principles such as provenance and original order.

rent need, the collection's value to the organization, and the amount of time and work necessary to organize the materials. The necessary degree of arrangement and description should also be evaluated. Does the collection warrant item, file, or box-level treatment? Do parts of the collection or the different formats of material represented in the collection (e.g., photographs, oral history tapes) warrant different levels of control?

Figure 6-3. Processing area at the Bentley Historical Library of the University of Michigan.

The initial archival inventory/survey and the transfer/accession form should establish series level control over archival materials. Arrangement is the process of determining and deciding on the proper physical arrangement of materials. In doing this, archivists also learn about the origin of the records and the originating office, thus gaining some intellectual control over the materials. Description is the further development of a written guide about the archival materials, which places the records in a historical and organizational context and includes information concerning the content and arrangement of the materials.

Prior to commencing arrangement and description activities, it is most appropriate and realistic for an archivist to arrange and describe materials with the aim of creating a box list or perhaps even a file-folder list for each series. Archivists recognize that the arrangement and description of archival materials is just one aspect of archival management and that it must

be balanced with all the other necessary functions of an archival program.

The best means of achieving intellectual control over an archival collection and providing the best information for all possible users is to work down. Following the Holmes model (see page 41), archivists should initially establish an overall brief understanding of the materials in the repository. Further arrangement and description should build on this understanding and constantly refine that knowledge through more in-depth analysis of the records. Much is lost if an archivist concentrates on one series in great depth and neglects other series or collections.

Archivists begin the process of organization by arranging the materials for use. When approaching a new collection or a recently accessioned records series, carefully study the entire group of records. The detail of this survey will necessarily be different if the collection numbers one box or two thousand boxes. The goal of this exercise, however, is to formulate an idea of the total scope and the different arrangement patterns within the whole.

- Are there subdivisions within the larger group?
- Are there different arrangements for these different subseries?
- Is there a discernable order which can be maintained?

These questions should be automatically answered as an archivist approaches a new series for the arrangement process.

In general, the archivist should disturb the original order of the records as little as possible. File-folder headings and internal divisions should also be maintained, if possible. In addition to providing a ready-made arrangement, the organization (or disorganization of records) can tell much about the workings of a person or organization. Arranging records for ease of use and increased access sometimes necessitates disregarding original order, but this should only occur with hesitation and after careful analysis. The reorganization of collections should only take place after close examination and consultation has failed to reveal an apparent order and research use can only be facilitated through reorganization.

The Finding Aid: Description

Once the arrangement of a record series is completed the detailed descriptive work can begin. Notes taken during arrangement can be useful in developing a written account of the content of the series and in analyzing the value of the records to certain types of researchers. These notes will also be valuable in compiling a brief history of the creator for inclusion in the finding aid.

DESCRIPTION is the development of written information concerning archival materials, such as the context in which records were created and the content of the records.

Archives employ different methods and levels of providing descriptions of materials for researchers. These include a repository guide, the descriptive finding aid, and various computer databases. A card catalog can be used to guide researchers to more detailed descriptive tools such as a computer database or a written finding aid, but it is these latter two which provide researchers with the most comprehensive information concerning the organization and contents of collections. The descriptive finding aid (either written or computerized) is

Table of Descriptive Products*

Level	Product
Repository	Guide Brochure
Record Group/ Collection	Inventory Accession Record
Series	Organizational History Functional Analysis of Office Biography
Contents	Description Notes
File Unit	Folder or Container List
Item	Calendar

*Robert Sink, March 1991

the most appropriate tool for guiding researchers to archival records.

Archival materials are best described by written or computerized finding aids. The finding aid combines the box or file-folder list with a written description of the records. Information gathered in the descriptive process should be added to any notes made at the time of surveying or accessioning to create a finalized description which meets professional standards. The finding aid serves as the primary means of intellectual access to the records. A finding aid contains two major sections:

1. A primarily narrative section orienting the researcher to a collection and
2. A list of the files or containers.

Elements of these two sections are outlined in Table 6-1.

Policies and Procedures Manual

Every archival repository should establish policies as well as procedural guidelines for performing all archival duties. Consistency in procedures makes training new staff less cumbersome. A detailed listing of functional steps in accessioning or the creation of finding aids, for example, also diminishes the number of errors or omissions in the final product. The establishment of procedures also ensures consistency in spite of staff changes.

A policies and procedures manual contains all policy statements and forms used by the archives or historical agency; guidelines and principles for major archival functions, such as reference and processing; and detailed notes on all stages in the handling of archival materials within a repository. The Procedures section should follow that outlined by Fredric M. Miller

Table 6-1. Major Sections of a Finding Aid

A. Explanation of the records (history and contents notes) including :

- Identification of the creator / compiler
- A title of the series (supplied by either the creator or the archivist)
- Inclusive and bulk dates of materials in the records
- The amount of materials (in a standard measurement, either linear feet or meters)
- Information on any subseries or the organization of the collection (alphabetical, chronological, by case number, etc.)
- A narrative which contains a history of the office or organization,
- A description of the office functions, procedures, activities that led to the creation of the records,
- Information concerning the contents of the records, surprises concerning materials found, disappointments concerning materials one would expect to be there but are not, etc.
- A container or perhaps a file list and descriptions of any series and subseries,
- A note concerning any restrictions on the records
- Notes concerning the condition in which the records were found (degree of reorganization, the destruction of provenance, preservation problems) and
- Data concerning the existence of complementary materials
- Citations to published works which have cited the collection or which would assist the researcher in working with the collection
- Name of the person who processed the collection
- Location of the materials

B. A brief listing the collection providing all box or folder headings.

in his recent *Arranging and Describing Archives and Manuscripts.*

Computer Applications in Archives

A computer is essential for today's archives and there are many types of software with archival applications. A basic wordprocessing system can save hours of retyping in the development of finding aids. Database management systems have also been employed in administering archival repositories, such as in the area of maintaining financial records or accession files. A computer format has also been designed specifically for the exchange of archival information. This is the United States Machine Readable Cataloguing for Archival and Manu-

Figure 6-4. The archivist enters descriptive information into a customized archival database following the instructions in the procedures manual of the Kraft General Foods Archives.

USMARC AMC is the acronym for the United States Machine Readable Cataloguing for Archival and Manuscripts Control. It is a computer format and is available on software for personal computers, on library systems, and national bibliographic networks. There are two national bibliographic databases in the United States. One is the Research Libraries Information Network (RLIN), which contains the records of major research libraries in the United States as well as the holdings of several state archives and special collections. The other is the Online Computer Library Center (OCLC) which contains the bibliographic records of many college and university libraries and public libraries throughout the United States.

scripts Control or USMARC AMC format. It is a format which prescribes a specific arrangement of data. In itself it is not a software program. The USMARC AMC format can be employed in various software programs, on local bibliographic databases, as well as in the national bibliographic utilities.

However, one need not have a computer to use the USMARC AMC format. In its simplest form, this format is a means of collecting standardized information to describe archival records. The USMARC AMC format is a descriptive tool, containing the same elements, described above, found in a well-constructed survey or finding aid. Once standardized information is consistently collected by an archives, this data can easily be coded for entry into a computer program, system, or utility which uses the USMARC AMC format. Standardized information should be routinely collected, even if an archives cannot afford computerization at the present time. This data can later be entered easily into a computer system.

Several applications of the USMARC AMC format include administrative functions such as tracking donor records and searching capabilities for locating specific materials. After consistently entering information in the USMARC AMC format into a computer, an archivist can determine how many linear feet of materials were accessioned during the past six months, who is responsible for processing a certain collection, or which collections are high priorities for conservation treatments. Use of a USMARC AMC based program or system can also assist in reference queries. Reports generated can be as diverse as how many collections were processed during a given year to updated internal location guides.

Another important use of the USMARC AMC format is that an archives can exchange information with other archives about their holdings, retention schedules, and preservation practices.

7

Reference and Access

Records exist to be used, and reference service is the range of activities archivists perform to facilitate use of archival materials. Arrangement and description of archival materials is not an end in itself but should facilitate retrieval of archival records and provide tools which assist users. The reference function is the one through which most people (e.g., the general public, co-workers, and superiors in an

---

REFERENCE SERVICE includes all the processes involved in assisting internal or external researchers to use archival records.

---

organization) come into contact with archivists. It is the one by which most archivists are judged and evaluated. In an institutional archives a majority of the use of archival materials is by internal users — the archivist's co-workers and superiors. Mary Jo Pugh's manual, *Providing*

Reference Services for Archives and Manuscripts, provides detailed descriptions of reference activities in different archival situations.[12] Her volume also describes sound reference practices, policies, and procedures.

Reference

People use archival materials for a variety of reasons. Administrators examine records documenting past decisions. Some individuals require proof of birth or baptism to get a drivers' license or social security benefits. A new homeowner may need information or pictures of the house from the past to restore structural elements. A physical plant manager will arrive at the archives one morning looking for blueprints to repair an electrical problem. Genealogists search through church records, land records, and census documents looking for clues concerning their ancestors. Academic historians examine whole groups of records to reconstruct communities—socially, politically, and physically. Most people come to the archives with an immediate problem to solve. Their questions

Figure 7-1. Research and reference area at the Moorland-Spingarn Research Center of Howard University.

and knowledge of the archival records, however, may be vague. It is not the role of the archivist to know the answer, but it is the job of the archivist to assist the researcher in locating the information that will provide the answers.

Internal researchers comprise the largest proportion of users for most institutional or organizational archives. The relationship between the archivist and internal users is different than the relationship between the archivist and external users, who are often trained historians. Administrators want the correct files or information in a very timely manner. Administrators rely on the archivist's knowledge of the collections, the archivist's research abilities, and the archivist's ability to analyze the sources of information. Administrators want the best source of information, not all the possible information on a topic. Institutional archivists, as employees of their organization, do undertake research projects and answer questions that involve the analysis of the archival materials in their care.

Reference is sometimes an art and at other times an inexact science. Upon entering an archives for the first time, an external researcher, i.e., one not employed by the organization spon-

soring the archives, should fill out a "Researcher Application" (see Appendix C for sample form) and receive a copy of the rules and regulations of the archives. For all patrons, whether internal to the organization or external, the archivist brings archival materials to the researcher and monitors the researcher during the use of the materials. Unlike library stacks where patrons select and retrieve books and other materials for themselves, storage areas in archives are closed to all researchers.

Each new researcher should also be interviewed by the archivist. This reference interview is often essential to the success of an archival search. Users do not always phrase questions clearly and concisely. More often, a user will ask to see one type of document which they think will answer the question at hand, when in reality another source would provide the required information. The reference interview is essential in finding the question behind the question. It is also a way for the archivist to reinforce particular rules, to evaluate the research skills of the user, and to determine the amount of assistance a researcher will need. Some researchers may not have much experience using archival materials and the archivist

Figure 7-2. Reference room personnel responding to telephone information requests at the New York City Department of Records and Information Services.

Figure 7-3. The reference archivist provides assistance to a researcher at the Austin History Center of the Austin Public Library.

may be required to provide some background for the users as they encounter primary resources for the first time. Provisions must be made for users desiring photocopies of documents or the reproduction of photographs, microforms, audio or video tapes, or film. (Sample forms for photocopies and for duplication of photographs are shown in Appendix D and E.)

A warning on copyright restrictions from 1976 Copyright Law should be clearly posted in the archives and on any photocopy machines. Users should be required to fill out and sign a separate form for the reproduction of materials in any form. The materials to be reproduced should be listed on this form. The institution should also decide if researchers are allowed to do their own

WARNING CONCERNING COPYRIGHT RESTRICTIONS

The 1976 Copyright Law of the United states (Title 17, U.S. Code) governs the making of photocopies or other reproductions of copyrighted material. Under conditions specified in the law, libraries and archives are authorized to furnish reproductions. One of these conditions is that the reproductions are not to be used for any purpose other than private study, scholarship, or research. If a user makes a request for, or later uses, any type of reproduction for purposes in excess of "fair use," that user may be liable for copyright infringement.

The Archives reserves the right to refuse to accept a copying order if in its judgement, fulfillment of the order would involve violation of U.S. Copyright Law.

photocopying or if all photocopying will be done by members of the archival staff. Allowing users to do their own photocopying is both a time saving and cost effective measure, however, the archivist should monitor all photocopying to ensure that users are aware of proper handling techniques for archival materials.

Each archives must also decide if additional permission is required for researchers who wish to quote directly from the collection. Permission to use an archival collection does not automatically imply the right to quote from or reproduce materials from a collection, although it is very difficult, if not impossible to monitor citation of materials after the users leaves the archives.

Charges for copies should be established before any requests are received by the archives. These charges should include the overhead costs of a copy machine, paper, preparation charges, and staff time. Most archives pass along these costs to researchers. Archives may also want to differentiate between researchers and commercial users, who may intend to use an image on a calendar or a book jacket. In the case of commercial users, an added publication fee may also be appropriate. The archivist should also determine a standard citation form for researchers to use when materials from an archives are quoted. This citation form should be clear enough so that the archivist can readily trace footnote entries for future users.

The archivist should monitor all reference use and keep detailed statistics. Use of the archives, including onsite researchers, visitors, telephone inquiries, and correspondence should be counted. Statistics provide evidence to present to budget committees for salary, personnel, and supply increases. They also demonstrate the services provided by the archives to an organization. Statistics aid archival personnel in monitoring the use and sometimes the overuse of collections. This information can assist the archivist in setting priorities for processing collections, preservation planning, organizing and implementing of a microfilming project, developing ideas for outreach programs, and protecting archival materials from theft.

Access

Access refers to rules and regulations that every archival program must establish to monitor or restrict use of particular materials. Whatever access restrictions are established should be applied equally to all researchers. Inconsistent treatment of researchers is unethical and can result in legal problems for a historical records program. In institutional archives, there will also be different access policies for internal employees and for outside researchers. Em-

Figure 7-4. Reference service includes providing access to archival materials in a variety of media. Shown here is a researcher using a videotape at the Austin History Center, Austin Public Library.

ployees of an organization may be required to use restricted materials to complete company projects. (The personnel director may need to refer to a former employee's personnel record to verify retirement benefits.)

An access policy is an essential document for all archival programs. It is comprised of three elements :

1. A statement regarding who can use certain materials.

2. A listing of restrictions (preferably by series).

3. Information concerning access to unprocessed records (such as, materials which have been accessioned, but for which full arrangement and descriptive treatment has not been completed).

Access policies should avoid blanket restrictions on collections, such as, "All materials are closed for a period of ten years after creation." Each series should be examined individually and restricted or opened on the basis of its own contents. Restrictions should be based on the presence of materials protected by laws (e.g., personnel records, student records, adop-

Figure 7-5. Another researcher is using the microfilm reader for his reference needs. Archival staff must be knowledgeable of all media and its corresponding hardware. Austin History Center, Austin Public Library.

tion records); the presence of personal information or personnel evaluations; and the sensitivity of issues raised in the records.

The sensitivity of some archival records decreases with the passage of time. Materials marked confidential twenty years ago usually contain little, if any, sensitive or secret information today. Sometimes, one even wonders what was so confidential in a letter when it was restricted. Other materials concern living individuals and the information contained in these letters may cause harm to those individuals. Restricting access to collections, however, should not be done simply because certain series or documents do not show the institution at its best.

8

Outreach

Archivists continually reach out to wide audiences of individuals who are affected by recordkeeping practices and the records themselves. Outreach is more than doing public programs and mounting exhibits. In face, some of the most effective means of outreach are the archivist's less-visible activities. Providing reference services, as described earlier (Chapter 7), is a form of outreach. Yet, so are the chance encounters at the water fountain, an annual budget review, or a meeting in the office of the company president. Each of these instances provides opportunities for outreach to different constituencies of users. Simply stated, outreach is any opportunity that the archivist has to provide service or promote use and awareness of the collections. Therefore, all archival functions—administrative, collection development, records management, reference work, and preservation—contain an aspect of outreach and should all be considered when planning outreach activities.

An effective outreach program adds strength and stability to any archival program.

Outreach can take on many forms. For example, encouraging greater use of the collections by administrators is one type of outreach activity. Yet, it is only one part of an effective outreach program that concerns relations with other departments. Other types of outreach might include increasing records management activities, providing assistance and insight into office automation, or studying how administrators in an organization use archival information to better plan for reference service. Constant contact with users helps archivists design effective outreach programs that are well received and popular with the targeted user's group.

Outreach activities include tangible products such as written reports, brochures, or repository guides. When developing outreach products, the archivist should have a specific audience in mind. Different archival constituencies have varying interests in the archives. For example, the archivist's supervisor in an institution will respond to an annual report that demonstrates archival activities and the archivist's carrying out of his or her responsi-

Figure 8-1. A meeting of an archival "Friends" organization at the Bentley Historical Library, University of Michigan.

Figure 8-2. Public programming includes lectures such as the Second Annual Dorothy Porter Wesley Lecture at the Moorland-Spingarn Research Center. Ms. Wesley is at the podium.

bilities over the past year. Other department heads are interested in the services the archives provides to support their on-going programmatic activities, such as reference service or records management.

External users are interested in how much they can learn about the archives prior to the actual research visit. Background research on collections has been done traditionally through published guides. Computers and telecommunications capabilities have changed this. Through remote access by computers, researchers can connect to online public access catalogs or bibliographic networks which provide de-

scriptive information concerning collections and Gopher software servers which can mount entire finding aids or actual images of documents or photographs from archives around the world.

In starting an archives, no program can implement all of these activities in the first year. However, the major constituencies should be identified and the initial outreach products should be geared to the need of the majority of the users.

Outreach activities can also take on the form of assisting key groups of external researchers in using the archives. Major groups

━━*SUMMER 1991*

OSU RECORD

Newsletter of the University Archives

RECORDS DISASTER

Early on the morning of June 10th, 1991, vandals and arsonists claiming membership in the radical animal rights organization, ALF or Animal Liberation Front, forced entry into the grounds and facilities of the OSU Mink Research Center. During this early morning raid, a barn containing animal feed and equipment was burned. The Center's administrative building which contained a laboratory, office space, research stations, and the office of the director was extensively vandalized. The walls were painted with threats and slogans. Large quantities of records and printed research materials were damaged with water and chemicals. Some of the records reportedly were stolen by the perpetrators of the attack.

Upon completion of the fire control activities and police investigation, the staff of the University Archives and Records Management Program assisted the staff of the Mink Research Center in the salvage and recovery of the records damaged during the attack. During the previous month, University Archivist Michael Holland and Assistant Uni-

Photo by Mark Floyd, News & Information.
Disaster recovery in progress at the OSU Animal Science Department Mink Farm.

versity Archivist Larry Landis had presented a disaster recovery workshop to Pacific Northwest records managers and archivists in Portland, and they were able to apply their recently refreshed skills in a real disaster situation. All available Archives staff members were put to work on Tuesday morning, June 11, in assessing the damage and salvaging the records. They worked on the site of the disaster for four days.

The situation which faced the Archives staff was not typical of most water related records disasters. In this disaster there was concerted human effort expended in destroying the records and in disarranging the original file order. When a pipe breaks, or other unintentional accidents occur, records, while damaged, are not intentionally shuffled. When disruption of records and information is the intent of the attack, records recovery becomes more labor and time intensive.

The Archives crew brought fans into the facility to establish air circulation throughout the office areas to delay the appearance of mold and mildew. When water damages records, the recovery workers usually have between 24 and 72 hours, depending upon temperature and humidity, before mold and mildew begins to grow and destroy wet records.

Monofilament nylon fishing line was strung throughout the facility to hang-dry some of the less badly damaged and less wet records. Good air circulation in the facility and adequate space to line-dry and air-dry records, off-prints and

Continued on page 4

Figure 8-3. The Oregon State University Archives keeps the university community, users, and donors aware of its activities through a newsletter.

of external users might include genealogists, business historians, parish historians, or local historians. The archives might sponsor a workshop for one of these groups, such as genealogists, which outlines the resources for doing family history in the archives. The workshop might also suggest research strategies to some groups with less experience in using archival materials.

Whenever archival materials are loaned out, an agreement should be prepared to avoid any confusion concerning responsibility and terms of the loan. A sample agreement is shown in Appendix F.

The number and types of outreach activities are plentiful. Other common examples include exhibits focusing on the repository's holdings, sponsorship of a symposium that highlights the research potential of the collections, or media programs featuring the products of research use of the archives.

Outreach is done when potential donors of archival materials are contacted, whether those donors are external to the organization or internal department heads. Each contact made by the archivist leaves an impression of the archives and archivists.

Also, friends' groups, volunteers, or an advisory board are important venues for outreach activities. Some archival programs have suc-

cessful "friends" groups who contribute monetarily to the upkeep of the archives or enable the archives to undertake special programs. Volunteers can provide an important means of expanding archival services and carrying out activities that would otherwise have taken years to complete. Advisory boards provide essential information to the archivist about the institutional culture and can provide support for difficult archival decisions. Friends, volunteers, and an advisory board all widen the circle of contacts for the archives and can provide essential support for an archival program. Each acts in a different way, but at their best, each type of support group can give added authority and initiative to the archival program. These groups are an important method of outreach and can result in closer ties within a community or institution and more support for the archives. The dynamics of an advisory board, discussed previously (Chapter 4), can also increase knowledge, support, and use of the archival program.

While a beginning archival program may not be able to plan and implement large-scale outreach activities, a brochure, discussions with other department heads, and an exhibit are modest activities with which to begin. These small beginnings are essential to the process of building a strong institutional or local base for the archival program.

9

The Archival Facility and Preservation

Archival records require special housing and handling to ensure their continued availability for future generations. The archives' physical plant should be designed to facilitate both the administration of the archival program, preservation planning activities, and use of archival records. To do this, the archivist must become knowledgeable of the archives' physical plant and learn how to best manage it. Preservation refers to the daily activities associated with the handling and storage of archival materials. Archival knowledge changes rapidly in the area of preservation and it is essential for the archivist to be aware of the most current research in this field. Conservation is physical treatment of an item or group of materials.

Site Selection: The Macro Environment

Few organizations can build their own archives building. Thus, the challenge is usually to renovate an existing area for the archival program. There is no perfect place to situate an archives in a building, but some sites offer greater advantages than others. Once the size of the area required has been determined, the focus turns to other important physical characteristics for a potential archives space (temperature, humidity, light, susceptibility to floods) which must be considered for effective management.

In designing or selecting an archives area, space should be allocated for

- Growing archival storage needs.
- Professional and technical staff.
- Research and reference services.

The size of the area needed can be reliably approximated by examining the present and estimated future staff size and responsibilities, research use, and potential amount of archival materials—both in the archives and those discovered as a result of the records survey and any subsequent records scheduling. The final site selected should be able to accommodate growth

---

PRESERVATION is the on-going mainte-nance of archival materials through proper storage and handling to ensure their sur-vival for use. CONSERVATION means phys-ically treating materials.

---

in the archival collection, staff, and research use.

It is most difficult to estimate the rate of growth of an archival collection, especially in the first few years after the establishment of an archival program, when a greater volume of material is identified as having enduring value and transferred to the archives. The amount of space needed also differs depending on the type of shelving used.

- Standard records center shelving,
- High-density double-depth shelving,
- Compact mobile shelving,
- Standard office shelving, or
- File cabinets.

Any shelving chosen should be at least 18-20 gauge metal shelving with a baked enamel finish. Each shelf should be able to hold between 150 and 200 pounds of archival mate-rials. All shelving should be securely assembled according to its own technical specifications and fastened to the floor or walls to increase its stability. Shelving designed for the specific type of archival or records storage boxes em-ployed in an archives is the most space efficient. File cabinets are the least efficient method of storage because of the space required to open the drawers. To maximize space, it is best to use a few standard box sizes for materials in one repository. The stack area must also allow for aisles (not less than 32 inches) which will ac-commodate carts and ladders in the stacks.

Space for a table and a telephone for short reference requests or to review documents without bringing them into the main office area is also preferable.

Archivists require a significant amount of space to process archival materials. Standard workspace or office size for each staff member is 125 square feet. If the staff member is ex-pected to process materials in his or her office, the space should be increased by at least 50%. If not, a separate processing area should be established which allows each processor ap-proximately 75 square feet. Each researcher requires approximately 50 square feet. Addi-tionally, space should be allocated for a refer-ence area (e.g., reference desk, finding aids, secondary published sources) and perhaps ex-hibit space. This area should be well lighted, provide an atmosphere conducive to work, have clear sight lines to monitor researchers and guard against theft, and contain sufficient elec-trical capability to run computers, microfilm reader/printers, and all of the other equipment necessary for the functioning of the historical records program.

When investigating a site for the archival program a series of questions should be asked.

- What is the history of the area(s) under consideration?
- What is the physical layout of the area?
- Is there a loading dock nearby for ease in transferring archival materials?
- Is the floor strong enough to hold the weight of archival materials?
- Is it secure enough for archival materials?
- Can all of the exits be locked? Are any needed as fire exits that must remain open or can break-away bars with alarms be installed?
- Does the area receive direct sunlight at some point during the day which effects the temperature of the area?

- Does the area provide substantial space for all archival functions?
- Does the space provide adequate room for the growth of the archival collections?
- Has flooding occurred in the area?
- If the site under consideration is in the basement, what is the level of the water table under the building?
- Is the area near any sources of water, e.g. water pipes, bathrooms, janitorial closets?
- Is the area near or under a condenser for the building's air conditioning system?
- Has the area been a site of infestation by silverfish, roaches, mice?

Political questions such as, "Will the placement of the archives help or hinder the mission of the program?" are also important to consider.

- Is the archives too far from other administrative offices or in an inconvenient location within the building?
- Can these obstacles be overcome through outreach?
- What are the local building and fire codes?
- Is there access for the disabled?

Although it is not recommended to select a site for the archival program with potential dangers from fire, flooding, or infestation, archivists can take steps to mitigate against these disasters if a less than ideal site must be selected. For example, if it is not possible to locate the archives away from potential flooding hazards such as restrooms, kitchens, cleaning closets, heating systems, and air-conditioning ventilation towers, precautionary measures against water damage should be taken. A water detection system can be installed and linked to a central fire or security system. The archivist should also store the archival materials at least four to six inches off of the ground.

Preservation Planning and Archives Site Preparation

Once a site has been selected, the planning for renovation and the equipping of the archives begins. A stable physical environment and strong administrative policies and authority are equally important in developing an enduring archival program. Regulation and stabilization of the environment are the most important investments that can be made to preserve archival materials. Monies spent in the beginning to stabilize temperature and relative humidity will be saved later through fewer conservation treatment needs.

Ideal conditions vary for different media of archival materials. The optimum conditions for archival paper records are between 55-65° Fahrenheit and between 30-40% relative humidity. Recent research has demonstrated that lower temperatures and relative humidity are best for all media represented in today's archival collections. It is most important, however,

Figure 9-1. A recording hygrothermograph measures temperature and humidity 24 hours a day at the Austin History Center, Austin Public Library.

to guard against the daily or weekly fluctuations in temperature and relative humidity that are common in many buildings. These fluctuations occur especially in buildings that are closed for the weekend. The key is to find the lowest possible temperature and relative humidity that an archives can maintain consistently, 24 hours a day, 365 days a year. As a first step in climate control, organizational archives should aim at achieving a stable temperature of 72º and a stable percentage between 35% and 55% relative humidity. Since stability is vitally important, these conditions should not vary more than 2-3% during any 24-hour period.[13] Mary Lynn Ritzenthaler's *Preserving Archives and Manuscripts,* a part of SAA's Archival Fundamentals Series, provides basic essential information on archival preservation.[14]

The best method of ensuring constant temperature and humidity in the archives is to purchase a separate heating, ventilation, and air-conditioning (HVAC) or environmental control unit for the archives. Many of these are designed for areas housing mainframe computers. An independent unit can then be used continuously, even when the system in the rest of the building is shut off at night, weekends, or during semester breaks. While the initial capital investment in an independent unit is more expensive than other options, the cost is far less than future restoration or conservation expenses for archival records and books stored in an unstable and unregulated environment. Archival planners should argue strongly for an independent HVAC unit.[15]

Environmental control units require accessibility to a roof or outside wall for an external ventilation.

If a separate environmental control system is not purchased for the historical records area, steps can be taken to improve storage conditions. Such measures include the installation of separate temperature controls for the archives area(s); changing the filters in the building's heating and cooling systems more frequently to diminish the dust and pollutants in the air; and purchasing an air conditioner, dehumidifier, or humidifier as needed. In all instances, the archives' temperature and relative humidity should be monitored and recorded regularly by precise instruments. The instruments which measure temperature and relative humidity are a recording thermohygrometer, a hygrometer, a battery-driven or sling psychrometer, or one of the new digital instruments.

Ultraviolet rays from the sun and fluorescent lights contribute to documentary deterioration, by causing ink to fade and paper to become brittle. Newspaper left in direct sunlight begins to change color within a matter of days. Exposing archival areas to direct sunlight should be avoided not only because of the ultraviolet light, but also because the intense heat makes it more difficult to regulate the internal temperature of an area. Ideally, all archival and rare books storage areas should be windowless. (However, the archives office should project a cheery, welcoming environment.) If windows are unavoidable, they should be heavily draped and the glass should be treated to filter out ultraviolet light. Some window glass breaks when this filtering material is applied, so the glass manufacturer should be contacted to ascertain whether the glass can withstand this process.

Ultraviolet light filters should be placed on all fluorescent lights in areas where archival records or rare books are stored, displayed, processed, or researched. Filters should be carefully checked for cracks when fluorescent lights are changed and then either changed or replaced, as necessary, on the new light. There is no visible difference in the amount of light or color of filtered ultraviolet light.

Regular housekeeping is also essential in the archives. Archival containers should be

Figure 9-2. Files in storage at the Kraft General Foods Archives. Note the sprinkler heads for a dry-pipe sprinkler system.

dusted and floors should be washed regularly. The filters in the HVAC system should also be checked every three months during the initial year of operation and at least every six months in later years. Draped windows are a source of dust and can necessitate an increased frequency of housekeeping.

Archivists should be alert to any signs of animal and insect infestation, such as animal droppings or small piles of wood or paper shavings. The archives should not be located near any staff lounges or trash receptacles, and the archives staff should not be allowed to eat in records storage areas. All garbage should be removed at night to limit the possibility of infestation by rodents or insects. New archival materials should be carefully examined during accessioning for infestation, mold, or mildew which can spread to previously unaffected archival materials, under some conditions, if not checked.

Fire prevention is a major concern in an archival facility. The archives should not be located near kitchen ovens, boilers, incinerators, smoking lounges, or other sources of heat and fire. Therefore, the most fireproof area should be selected for the archives and fire-resistant walls, floors, and doors should be installed. Smoke detectors, preferably linked to a security service or the local fire department, are essential. Individual smoke detectors cannot be heard afterhours in most offices.

The archivist should also have some knowledge of the fire suppression system used in the building and the location of its shutoff mechanisms. Traditional water-based sprinkler systems are the most cost-effective and viable fire suppressants available for most archival repositories. While water damage can be harmful to records, conservation techniques for restoring water-damaged materials have improved in recent years. If a sprinkler system is installed, possible water damage can be minimized by employing a dry pipe system with on-off or independently operating sprinkler heads. Although there is a delayed reaction time with a dry pipe system (one in which water is not constantly sitting in the pipes), dry pipes do eliminate possible damage to records if a malfunction or a leak occurs. Dry pipes should be flushed periodically to avoid the accumulation of rust or corrosion. On-off heads are preferable because they discharge only in the region of a fire and shut off automatically when the conflagration is suppressed. In wet pipe systems without on-off heads, the entire system drains when a fire is detected anywhere and remains on until the water supply is exhausted.

Carbon dioxide, which is employed in A-B-C fire extinguishers, is another effective method of fire suppression. Although it is better than water for both archival records and rare books, carbon dioxide diminishes the oxygen in the air to a lethal level for humans. Its use is generally restricted to handheld fire extinguishers. Carbon dioxide should not be used in areas where certain chemicals are housed, such as those common in an in-house micrographics operation. In these areas, halon extinguishers are still considered standard.

Halon (halogenated hydrocarbon) gas systems were formerly thought to be excellent for fire suppression in archives because they did not harm paper and other media. Halon suppresses the fire by interfering with the combustion cycle and while it suppresses the actual flames, it is less effective with smoldering fires. However, halon employs chlorofluorocarbons that have been determined to be detrimental to the ozone layer.

A final issue is security of the collection. Keys to archives areas should be strictly limited to archives personnel, security officers, and perhaps the physical plant. Afterhours access by maintenance staff may be limited to office and research areas. Research space should be monitored. Storage areas should be off-limits to all persons except the archives staff. Doors leading into the office, work, and storage areas should be visible to a member of the archives staff at all times. It is also necessary to ask all persons, such as the physical plant staff, to notify archives personnel prior to entry into the storage area, except in the case of an emergency.

Preservation: The Micro Environment

In addition to maintaining control over the macro environment, archivists must also work to preserve the micro environment of their collections. Different media of archival materials have different storage requirements. The following paragraphs contain a brief review of the properties and optimum storage environment for different media: paper, photographs, sound recordings, motion picture films, audio and video tapes, and electronic media.

Paper

Archival materials composed of paper are best stored in acid-free buffered, lignan-free file folders and boxes. In time, acid-free folders and boxes also become acidic and should be replaced. This is also why many archival supply manufacturers are now "buffering" their acid-free, lignan-free folders. These "buffered" fold-

---

ACID FREE is used to signify paper having a pH of 7.0 or higher. Today, acid-free file folders and boxes are often buffered with an alkaline substance capable of neutralizing acids, buffering raises the pH to at least 8.5.

Figure 9-3. Compact mobile shelving at the Kraft General Foods Archives.

ers have a pH of 8.5 (regular acid-free, lignan-free folders have a pH of 7.0). The process of acidification of acid-free, lignan-free file folders and boxes takes longer in the buffered folders.

Archival boxes and baked enamel shelving are preferable to file cabinets as a permanent method of storage for paper-based records and artifactual materials. When the space needed to open the drawers is considered, file cabinets use more space than shelving with archival boxes. Wood shelving contains many vapors and elements which can damage paper records. Although it is possible to seal wood shelving, this is a difficult process and if done incorrectly, can further harm archival materials.

Photographs

Photographs are best stored individually, in chemically stable polyester sleeves. Photographic positives and negatives should be stored separately. Types of stable polyester are

LIGNAN is an element in wood now thought by preservation experts to be a major cause of deterioration in paper. Acid-free, "lignan-free" file folders and boxes will last longer and take longer to acidify than plain acid-free supplies.

mylar, polypropylene, and polyethylene. Photographs stored under hot, humid conditions will stick to their enclosures, even if those enclosures are stable, polyester sleeves. Photographs are inherently unstable and are very expensive to maintain properly.

During accessioning or processing, the existence of any nitrate and early "safety film" negatives should be noted. An attempt should be made to segregate all nitrate negatives from the rest of the collection and some plan for the conversion of these negatives to safety film

Figure 9-4. Film storage area at the
Archives of the Evangelical
Lutheran Church in America.

should be developed. Nitrate negatives, used
roughly between 1920 and 1950, deteriorate
and can be very unstable and combustible if
stored in high temperature and humidity.

Motion Picture Film and Audio and Video Tapes

Motion picture film is ideally stored at very
cold temperatures and acclimated slowly prior
to viewing. Currently, film curators are debat-
ing the optimum mode of storage for motion
picture film. Issues in this debate include hori-
zontal versus vertical storage, and plastic versus

metal canisters. The problems associated with
nitrate film also effect motion picture film.

Magnetic media such as audio and video
tapes also present different storage problems.
Video tapes are inherently unstable and predic-
tions are that their shelf life is approximately
twenty years. The image is attached to the tape
magnetically and unstable environmental conditions or electrical current can cause this bond
to break and erase the tape. Video tapes should
be stored upright with the tape on the bottom.
Audio and video tapes should be rewound periodically at a slow speed to maintain an even
amount of tension. Use of the fast forward and

fast rewind options are not recommended for any archival tapes. Audio tapes are not considered permanently viable. Therefore, in oral history collections the transcript is considered the permanent, archival record.

Digital Media

Electronic records (computerized data stored on tapes, disks, etc.) are becoming common accessions in archives. Their preservation and access problems go hand in hand. These have particular problems in terms of storage, handling, and use and often present the interesting problem of the archives not being able to review the materials without the aid of a specific computer system, documentation, or software program. If the electronic records warrant preservation, the archives must ensure that the records are accompanied by sufficient documentation on the computer processes used to generate the records. Electronic databases can often be stored as flat files. Digital text files and multimedia files, however, are often software dependent. This creates conversion problems for archivists. The newer the media, the more difficult it is to preserve, particularly since less is known about its optimal storage conditions. A good introduction to the issues surrounding electronic records is Charles M. Dollar's *Archival Theory and Information Technologies*.[16]

Motion picture films, audio and video tapes, and particularly electronic records are accessed through a variety of different types of machines. The archivist should make sure that equipment is available to recover the information from these media. In many cases, the archivist needs to convert the image, sound, or data to a medium that can now be retrieved more easily. Equipment obsolescence is an increasingly large problem for archivists.

In the case of these types of media, the original may be perfectly preserved, but the archivist may be unable to retrieve information from the records due to a lack of equipment.

Archival Supplies

In buying supplies, archivists should be wary. The word "archival" is solely an adjective and not a standard. Some products advertised as "archival" do nothing to preserve records. In buying boxes and file folders, archivists should buy only those which are identified as acid-free, acid-buffered, and lignan-free. If a photograph album is advertised as "archival," ask what type of plastic and paper is used. Some type of archival supplies, such as acid-free, lignan-free file products, have been tested by the American National Standards Institute (ANSI) and some catalogs give specific information concerning these test results.

Special Preservation Problems

The initial inventory and daily accessioning practices should reveal any major preservation problems, such as mold or infestation. Before any steps are taken to attack an infestation problem or remove mold, archival materials should first be appraised to determine their long-term value. If the archivist decides to retain damaged materials, immediate action should then be taken to isolate them from all other archival materials. Mold damage is difficult to control and while it may become dormant for periods of time, it can reactivate in a warm, humid environment. In a muggy environment, mold will not only become active, but will migrate and infect previously undamaged materials.

Options for solving the mold problem and infestation are varied. Most are controversial, expensive and, if done improperly, can cause more damage to the records. Treatments include fumigation, freezing, and chemical treatment.

The archivist should also consider the alternatives to treatment of the original, such as photocopying, digital imaging, or microfilming the moldy or infested materials which can then be discarded. In this way, information can be preserved. The availability, cost, and feasibility of each of these options should be weighed against conservation treatments of any damaged materials.

Micrographics

Sometimes, the preservation of the information in archival records is more important than maintaining the physical records themselves. This is especially true in the light of other circumstances, such as lack of space, conservation problems, or the desire to provide increased availability of the documents at other repositories. In such cases, micrographics is an option.

Any microfilming project should be carefully planned and all goals and expectations should be outlined. Bids from several microfilm vendors should be solicited and a detailed contract should be agreed upon and signed by all parties. Agencies which fund microfilming projects require all grantees to produce a negative on silver halide film for permanent security storage, a duplicating negative, and a use copy. To be considered archival, silver halide film is now rated according to its life expectancy. This life expectancy (LE) rating was approved by the American National Standards Institute in Specification IT9.1 A.N.S.I.-1989.[17] The LE rating is determined by thiosulfite limits, image stability, and physical characteristics of the film. Silver halide film, exposed and developed according to IT9.1, can last up to five centuries *if stored under the optimal environmental conditions* discussed and enunciated in ANSI PH1.43-1983. Most archival facilities store the master security microfilm offsite at a carefully selected location that has appropriate tempera-

Figure 9-5. A technical support aide at the Municipal Archives of the City of New York inspects microfilm to ensure archival quality.

ture and relative humidity controls. The specifications for preservation microfilming are detailed in Nancy Gwinn, *Preservation Microfilming: A Guide for Librarians and Archivists* (Chicago: American Library Association, 1987).[18]

Micrographics has increased the availability of archival records and provides an alternative to restoration. Some records are destroyed after microfilming because they are deteriorating or because it is necessary to save storage space. The historical and legal issues surrounding destroying original materials should be carefully explored prior to any destruction of records after microfilming. Materials should be carefully selected for microfilming; not all materials merit retention through microfilming. Also, locating improperly organized materials on microfilm can be difficult.

Digital Imaging

Newly established programs will probably want to concentrate on automation through the description of collections in bibliographic networks such as OCLC or RLIN. However, other automated techniques are on the horizon. Digital imaging is a new technology that shows great promise for preserving information as well as increasing access to that information. Digital images have the potential for longevity in the sense that the images can be transported from one application to another with absolute fidelity, i.e., the images are not media dependent. Longevity is dependent, though, on sound project planning as well as the adoption of commonly used protocols and emerging standards for creating, compressing, and storing images. In considering any application of imaging technology, the archivist should ensure that the images can be migrated to conform with changes in hardware and software as new applications are developed. Any consideration of

the use of digital imaging must include plans for refreshing, upgrading, and storing the digital files to ensure accessibility over time.

Digital imaging is becoming a cost-effective alternative to microfilming or photocopying, although the costs of maintaining the images over time must be considered. Many state and local governments are moving toward digital imaging because of the flexibility it affords regarding access. International standards are under development at this time by the Association for Information and Image Management (AIIM) and the National Information Standards Organization (NISO). The National Association of Government Archives and Records Administrators (NAGARA) and the National Archives and Records Administration (NARA) have also issued guidelines for state governments considering imaging projects to increase access to records and as a means of storage.[19] The use of digital technology enables a user to call up images in a variety of ways, irrespective of the order in which the images were scanned. As with any microfilming project, the goals and objectives of an imaging project must be clearly established prior to selecting equipment or deciding on the technical requirements. Archivists in all institutions should watch developments in this area closely.

Conservation

Professional conservators can restore many documents thought to be beyond reclamation. However, the cost of repairing one item can be equal to the electricity costs of an HVAC system which controls the temperature and relative humidity and filters the air for the entire year. The initial focus of any archival program should be on preservation planning activities that benefit the entire collection (e.g., control of the temperature and relative humidity).

Figure 9-6. Archivist at the New York City Department of Records and Information Services (DORIS) processing water-damaged records of the New York City Department of Parks.

If any intensive restoration work is planned, a conservator should be chosen as carefully as an archivist. Several professional conservators should be consulted to evaluate recommended treatments and to compare costs. The quality of a conservator's work should never be judged solely on the appearance of a finished product. When an item is returned from a conservator, documentation concerning all chemicals and materials used during treatment should accompany the restored item, as well as before and after pictures. The American Institute for the Conservation of Historic and Artistic Works has recently initiated a program to recommend conservators in different areas of the country with various specialties.

10

Bibliographical Essay

Many journals and books deal with the issues facing archivists and other information professionals in the twentieth century and the concerns that will be faced in the twenty-first century. One of the best sources for these publications is the Society of American Archivists (see Chapter 11). The Society of American Archivists (SAA) has developed a new series of seven manuals entitled the *Archival Fundamentals Series* focusing on modern archival theory and practice. The series includes works on the nature of archival materials and treats the topics of appraisal, arrangement and description, and preservation. Another increasingly important source for bibliographies and information on current archival issues is the National Archives and Records Administration, Archives Library Information Center (ALIC), Washington, D.C. 20408.

Following is an annotated bibliography of archival materials. This bibliography does not attempt to be comprehensive. In general, it lists works that can be used to begin studying an archival topic, a specific medium of materials or a functional area of archival administration, or to further explore a point mentioned in this book. This bibliography also focuses on publications which are readily accessible. In most cases, a recent publication is listed not only on its merit, but because it provides the most comprehensive bibliography on a subject to date.

General Reference Sources / Bibliography

An essential work for understanding archival terminology is *The Glossary of Archivists, Manuscript Curators, and Records Managers,* by Lynn Lady Bellardo and Lewis Bellardo (Chicago: Society of American Archivists, 1992). This publication, part of SAA's Archival Fundamentals Series, defines terms used in the archival profession as well as in allied professions such as records management and information science.

Bibliographies demonstrate the wealth of writings available concerning archives and archival administration. For those seeking more information on a specific topic one of the following two bibliographies will provide assistance.

Frank B. Evans, *Modern Archives and Manuscripts: A Select Bibliography* (Chicago: Society of American Archivists, 1975), is a comprehensive bibliography of earlier archival works.

Richard J. Cox, *Archives and Manuscripts Administration: A Basic Annotated Bibliography* (Nashville, TN: American Association for State and Local History, 1989), AASLH Technical Report 14 is a more recent, yet selective, treatment of the archival literature.

A handy brochure which succinctly provides some guidelines for institutions intending to hire an archivist is "Guidelines for Selecting an Archivist" (Archivists Roundtable of Metropolitan New York and the Mid-Atlantic Regional Archives Conference, 1985).

Information on Starting Specific Types of Archives

Archival principles apply to all archival programs. However, specific types of archives face similar administrative systems, legal constraints, and problems which are dealt with in the following publications.

College and University Archives

Two recent books approach the development and management of college and university archives from different, complementary perspectives. These are William Maher, *The Management of College and University Archives* (Metuchen, NJ: SAA and Scarecrow Press,

1992), and Helen Samuels, *Varsity Letters: Documenting Modern Colleges and Universities* (Metuchen, NJ: SAA and Scarecrow Press, 1992).

State and Local Government Archives

The creation of the National Association of Government Archives and Records Administrators (NAGARA) in the 1980s has led to increased public awareness of the importance of state and local government records throughout the United States. The *NAGARA Guide,* listed in the self-assessment and planning section, is an example of this awareness and of the current steps being taken to improve these records. Bruce W. Dearstyne's *The Management of Local Government Records: A Guide for Local Officials* (Nashville, TN: American Association of State and Local History, 1988) is a good starting point for municipalities that want to establish control over records and ensure their preservation. An older classic article of interest is Margaret Cross Norton, "Organizing a New State Archives," *Norton on Archives,* Thornton W. Mitchell, ed. (Chicago: Society of American Archivists, 1979), pp. 39-52.

Business Archives

A good place to begin examining the world of business archives is with the recent publication *A Selected and Annotated Bibliography on Business Archives and Records Management* by Karen M. Benedict (Chicago: Society of American Archivists, 1992). Bruce Bruemmer and Sheldon Hochheiser's *The High Technology Company: An Historical Research and Archival Guide* (Minneapolis: Charles Babbage Institute, 1989), examines archival issues in a modern organization. The Society of American Archivists (Business Archives Section) has also printed a brochure entitled *Business Archives in North America* (1991) which is a helpful source of information. For a general overview of the issues facing business archivists, an older article is Joseph W. Ernst "The Business Archivist: Problems and Perspectives," *Business History Review,* 44 (Winter 1970), pp. 536-546.

Museum Archives

Museums have long recognized the need to establish the "provenance" of their art collections. Yet, many museums have archival materials that not only demonstrate the origin of their art collections but also provide information on artists and on the museum's own administrative processes, such as fundraising and community relations. *Museum Archives: An Introduction* by William A. Deiss (Chicago: Society of American Archivists, 1984) provides a general overview of an archival program in a museum setting.

Religious Archives

There are many small religious archives in North America. Two publications which address issues pertinent to the establishment, maintenance, and use of religious archives are James M. O'Toole's *Basic Standards for Diocesan Archives: A Guide for Bishops, Chancellors, and Archivists* (Chicago: Association of Catholic Diocesan Archivists, 1991) and Sr. Jo Ann Euper's "Starting a Religious Congregation Archives: Administrative Formulas for Better or Worse," *Midwestern Archivist,* 5 no. 1 (1980), pp. 21-28. These two works are both from the Roman Catholic tradition, yet the issues raised are pertinent to religious archives of all faiths. Shuster's article "Documenting the Spirit," *American Archivist* 45 (Spring 1982), pp. 135-141, is also an important article for archivists in religious collections to read.

Special Subject Collections

Special collections can be incorporated into the collecting policy of a newly established archives or can be the result of increased awareness of the gaps in certain types of documentation in an established archives. Two articles that specifically discuss the establishment of special subject collections in the areas of ethinic archives and the performing arts are noted below.

Dorothy L. Heinrich's article, "Establishing an Ethnic Collection in a Small Institution," *Midwestern Archivist* 2, no. 1 (1977), pp. 41-48, discusses the identification of just such a gap and the steps that the archives took in collecting materials in a new subject area.

Increased interest in the archives of performing arts organizations has led to the establishment of archives in individual organizations, such as symphony orchestras, as well as general collections documenting jazz or a specific musician. Carolyn A. Sheehy's article, "Chicago Dance Collection: A Case in *Pointe*," *American Archivist* 53 (Summer 1990, is a study of several organizations that chose not to care for their records but to donate them to another institution.

General Works on Archival Science

The Society of American Archivists has published a new series of manuals, the Archival Fundamentals Series, dealing with major archival functions (e.g., Arrangement and Description, Appraisal, and Reference). These manuals will be discussed in the appropriate category. The general introduction to this series is James M. O'Toole's book *Understanding Archives and Manuscripts* (Chicago: Society of American Archivists, 1990). *Understanding*

Archives and Manuscripts provides an excellent introduction to the other manuals as well as an insight into the evolution of archives in North America and some of the basic theoretical issues archivists confront.

Another general work which introduces archival administration and the variety of archival programs and questions faced by archivists is *A Modern Archives Reader: Basic Readings on Archival Theory and Practice*, edited by Maygene F. Daniels and Timothy Walsh (Washington, DC: National Archives Trust Board, 1984).

Two classic works on the care of historical records are T. R. Schellenberg, *Modern Archives: Principles and Techniques* (Chicago: University of Chicago Press, 1956) and Kenneth Duckett, *Modern Manuscripts: A Practical Manual for Their Management, Care, and Use* (Nashville, TN: American Association for State and Local History, 1975). Schellenberg will be more appropriate for institutional archives; Duckett focuses on collections of the private papers of individuals.

Archival Culture and the History of the Profession

F. Gerald Ham's article "The Archival Edge," *American Archivist* 38 (January 1975), pp. 5-13, was a seminal article and set the tone for the archival profession in the mid-1970s through the early 1980s. Later in the 1980s, the Goals and Priorities Task Force (GAP) of the Society of American Archivists awakened the archival profession to the increased need to heighten public awareness about the fragility and importance of historical materials, the necessity of greater cooperation between archivists, archival institutions, and allied professions, and the need to plan for the future. This report was entitled *Planning for the Archival Profession: A Report of the SAA Task Force on Goals and Priorities* (Chicago: Society of American Archivists, 1986).

The archival profession is active, evolving, and becoming more and more interested in documenting its development. David Bearman's "1982 Survey of the Archival Profession," *American Archivist* 46 (Spring 1983), pp. 233-239, is a good place to begin to see the diversity and trends in the archival profession. Michele F. Pacifico's article "Founding Mothers: Women in the Society of American Archivists, 1936-1972," *American Archivist* 50 (Summer 1987), pp. 370-389, provides insight into the degree to which women have always been an integral part of the archival profession.

A new entry into the debate over where the archival profession stands and where it is going is Richard J. Cox's *American Archival Analysis: The Recent Development of the Archival Profession in the United States* (Metuchen, NJ: Scarecrow Press, 1990).

Management and Program Evaluation

The need to adopt modern managerial techniques and establish goals and priorities for individual historical records programs has long been recognized. However, the number of useful publications solely on this topic grew substantially in the late 1980s. The publications listed below fall into two categories: more general works dealing with administrative issues and actual guides to planning or self-assessment.

Thomas Wilsted and William Nolte's *Managing Archival and Manuscript Repositories* (Chicago: Society of American Archivists, 1991) is a welcome addition to the basic archival bookshelf. It is a more in-depth treatment of the policies, documents, and principles mentioned in Chapter 4 of this book concerning the sound management of an archival program. Richard J. Cox's *Managing Institutional Archives: Foundational Principles and Practices* (Westport, CT: Greenwood, 1992), also provides basic information for organizational archives. Paul McCarthy's article "The Management of Archives: A Research Agenda" with a commentary by Thomas Wilsted, *American Archivist* 51 (Winter and Spring 1988), pp. 51-72, raises important issues for archival administrators to consider when building and directing a program. Gregory S. Hunter's article "Filling the Gap: Planning on the Local and Individual Levels," *American Archivist* 50 (Winter 1987), pp. 110-115, is a succinct and practical guide to the planning process. Elizabeth Yakel's "Institutionalizing an Archives: Developing Historical Records Programs in Organizations," *American Archivist* 52:12 (Spring 1989), pp. 202-207, discusses the role and image of archivists in small institutional archives.

Paul McCarthy's manual, *Archives Assessment and Planning Workbook* (Chicago: Society of American Archivists, 1989) leads an archival program step-by-step through the assessment and planning processes toward the formation of a realistic plan. Also, *Strengthening New York's Historical Records Programs: A Self Study Guide* (Albany, NY: State Archives and Records Administration, 1988) assists archival programs in the task of self-evaluation and contains clearly defined minimal standards for archives to follow.

Ethics

"The Code of Ethics for Archivists" (Chicago: Society of American Archivists, 1992) is the starting point for understanding the ethical issues which surround the archival profession. This publication gives both the code itself and a commentary. A general article which considers archival ethics in the context of professional organizations is David Horn's "The Development of Ethics in Archival Practice," *American Archivist* 52 (Winter 1989), pp. 64-71. Two other articles that examine archival ethics are Elena Danielson, "The Ethics of Access," *American Archivist* 52 (Winter 1989), pp. 52-62, and Nancy Lankford "Ethics and the Reference Archivist," *Midwestern Archivist* 8, no. 1 (1983).

Heather MacNeil's *Without Consent: The Ethics of Disclosing Personal Information in Public Archives* (Metuchen, NJ: SAA and Scarecrow, 1992) presents a comprehensive discussion of the legal and ethical issues surrounding privacy and access legislation in the United States and Canada.

Collection Development

F. Gerald Ham's article "Archival Choices: Managing the Historical Record in an Age of Abundance," *American Archivist* 47 (Winter 1984), pp. 11-22, sets the stage for any discussion of collection development and appraisal. It is essential reading for any archivist trying to document institutions or individuals in the twentieth (or twenty-first) century. Another thought-provoking article is Helen Willa Samuels' "Who Controls the Past?" *American Archivist* 49 (Spring 1986), pp. 109-124. This article discusses the effect of creation on archival records and the absolute necessity for archivists to work together to ensure that documentation in certain areas will exist for later generations.

Two articles which look specifically at the impact and common fallacies of collecting policies and collection development are Linda J. Henry's "Collecting Policies of Special-Subject Repositories," *American Archivist* 43 (Winter 1980), pp. 57-63, and Mary Lynn McCree's "Good Sense and Good Judgment:

Defining Collections and Collecting" in *A Modern Archives Reader*: *Basic Readings on Archival Theory and Practice,* ed. Maygene F. Daniels and Timothy Walsh (Washington, DC: National Archives Trust Board, 1984).

Finally, Robert Shuster's article "Documenting the Spirit," *American Archivist* 45 (Spring 1982) pp. 135-141, discusses the specific problems surrounding the documentation of religious experience.

Appraisal

Appraisal is an essential archival function; however, it is the most difficult to explain. F. Gerald Ham's new manual, *Selecting and Appraising Archives and Manuscripts* (Chicago: Society of American Archivists, 1992), synthesizes the theory and practice of appraisal in North American archives. This volume is part of Archival Fundamentals Series. In researching a means of quantifying the appraisal process, Frank Boles and Julia Marks Young, in "Exploring the Black Box: The Appraisal of University Administrative Records," *American Archivist* 48 (Spring 1985), pp. 121-140, have developed a set of questions archivists should ask during the appraisal process. Appraisal may or may not be quantifiable, however, their questions demonstrate the variety of considerations archivists should take into account during the appraisal process. Their entire study has been published as *Archival Appraisal* (New York: Neal Schuman, 1991).

The continuing necessity of appraisal and reappraisal is demonstrated in Leonard Rappaport's article, "No Grandfather Clause: Reappraising Accessioned Records," *American Archivist* 44 (Spring 1981), pp. 143-150. An opposing viewpoint is voiced by Karen Benedict, "Invitation to a Bonfire: Reappraisal and Deaccessioning of Records as Collection Management Tools in an Archives—A Reply

to Leonard Rapport," *American Archivist* 47 (Winter 1984), pp. 43-49.

How and why people create different groups of records has an impact on the appraisal process. The best example of how creation effects appraisal is in *Appraising the Records of Modern Science and Technology: A Guide* (Cambridge: Massachusetts Institute of Technology, 1985) by Joan K. Haas, Helen Willa Samuels, and Barbara Trippel Simmons .

Arrangement and Description

Arranging and Describing Archives and Manuscripts by Fredric M. Miller is part of the Archival Fundamentals Series (Chicago: Society of American Archivists, 1990). Miller clearly explains archival theory in these areas and demonstrates how these principles are applied in the archives.

A classic article is Oliver Wendell Holmes "Archival Arrangement—Five Different Operations At Five Different Levels," *American Archivist* 27 (January 1964, pp. 21-41). Finally, an article designed to help archivists set priorities for collections and process materials with effective use in mind is Megan Floyd Desnoyer, "When is a Collection Processed?" in *Midwestern Archivist* 7, no. 1 (1982), pp. 5-23.

Reference and Access

Mary Jo Pugh's vast experience in providing reference service in an archival setting is apparent in her writings on this subject. Her manual, *Providing Reference Services for Archives and Manuscripts,* also part of the Archival Fundamentals Series (Chicago: Society of American Archivists, 1992), is a comprehensive guide to all the responsibilities faced by reference archivists. Pugh's article "The Illusion of Omniscience: Subject Access and the

Reference Archivist," *American Archivist* 45 (Winter 1982), pp. 33-44, considers the means of overcoming the difficulties of archival reference. For a general synopsis of reference activities in different types of archival institutions, *Reference Services in Archives,* edited by Lucille Whalen and Bill Katz is a good choice. (New York: Haworth Press, 1986).

"Description and Reference in the Age of Automation," *American Archivist* 50 (Spring 1987), pp. 192-209, by Avra Michaelson is required reading for any archivist using computer applications in the archives or thinking about automating.

Outreach

Public programs and exhibits can be the bane of an archivists existence. However, the following two guides can assist archivists in developing public programs and exhibits which suit their institutions and their budgets. The first manual is Ann Pederson and Gail Casterline Farr, *Archives and Manuscripts: Public Programs* (Chicago: Society of Archivists, 1982); the second is *Archives and Manuscripts: Exhibits* (Chicago : Society of American Archivists, 1980), by Gail Casterline Farr.

More recently, outreach has been defined more broadly. Timothy L. Erickson's " 'Preoccupied with Our Own Gardens': Outreach and Archivists," *Archivaria* 31 (Winter 1990-91), pp. 114-122 best illustrates a broader conceptualization of outreach.

Legal Issues

The primer on legal issues relating to archives is Gary M. Peterson and Trudy Huskamp Peterson, *Archives and Manuscripts: Law* (Chicago: Society of American Archivists, 1985). This manual discusses laws relating to archives

such as copyright and provides samples of donation and deposit agreements which can easily be adapted to fit any institution. Trudy Huskapm Peterson, "The Deed and the Gift," *American Archivist* 42 (January 1979), pp. 61-66, treats the relationship between donors and archival repositories.

Donald S. Skupsky's *Recordkeeping Requirements* (Information Requirements Clearinghouse, 1988), provides insight into the legal basis of records retention, and disposition.

Automated Techniques for Online Description

Marion Matters' *Introduction to the USMARC Format for Archival and Manuscripts Control* (Chicago: Society of American Archivists, 1990), provides an overview of the purpose, history, and use of the MARC format.

Steven Hensen's *Archives Personal Papers and Manuscripts* (2nd edition) (Chicago: Society of American Archivists, 1989) applies the rules stated in the *Anglo-American Cataloguing Rules*, 2nd ed. to archival and manuscript materials. Hensen's work sets the standards for archival usage of the MARC AMC format. The Hensen manual, or APPM II as it is commonly called, is now in a second edition.

A final volume to note is Richard Smiraglia, ed., *Describing Archival Materials: The Use of the MARC AMC Format* (New York: Haworth Press, 1990).

Records Management

Ira A. Penn, Anne Morddel, Gail Pennix, and Kelvin Smith, *Records Management Handbook* (Brookfield, VT: Gower Publishing Co., 1989) provides an broad introduction to the concepts of records management.

Preservation, Conservation, and Disaster Planning

The Guide and Resources for Archival Strategic Preservation Planning (Atlanta: National Association of Government Archives and Records Administrators, 1990) combines three separate tools for self-evaluation, including a computer-assisted framework for institutional self-assessment and planning on preservation issues and a resource compendium of vendors, supplies, and services concerning preservation activities. Although published by an organization geared to improving governmental archives, the guide is useful in any type of archival program.

Preserving Archives and Manuscripts, by Mary Lynn Ritzenthaler (Chicago: Society of American Archivists, 1993) is another in the Archival Fundamentals Series. This manual gives current information on preservation research and discusses the best means of establishing preservation priorities and balancing preservation needs.

The Spring 1990 issue of the *American Archivist* is dedicated to preservation concerns. Among the series of fine articles in this volume are George M. Cunha, "Current Trends in Preservation, Research and Development," pp. 192-202, and Karen Garlick's "Planning an Effective Holdings Maintenance Program," pp. 256-264.

Another useful publication aimed at state archives is *Preservation Needs in State Archives* (Albany, NY: National Association of Government Archives and Records Administrators, 1986; reprinted 1988).

Disaster planning can mean the difference between losing an entire collection to a fire or flood or being able to save or recover significant portions of records. A manual which assists a repository in drafting its own disaster plan is

Judith Fortson, *Disaster Planning and Recovery: A How-to-do-it Manual for Librarians and Archivists* (New York: Neal-Schuman Publishers, 1992).

If interventive treatment of archival documents is necessary, the brochure "Selecting and Working with a Conservator: Conservation Services Referral System" (American Institute for the Conservation of Historic and Artistic Works, 1400 16th Street, NW, Suite 340, Washington DC 20036) is designed to assist repositories in choosing a reputable conservator.

Facilities Planning

Creating a user-friendly and preservation-conscious environment in which to administer archival records is difficult. So is locating information regarding the design of an archival facility. Therefore, Susan G. Schwartzburg and Holly Bussey work, *Libraries and Archives: Design and Renovation with a Preservation Perspective* (Metuchen, NJ: Scarecrow Press, 1991) is a welcome addition to the literature. William P. Lull, *Conservation Environment Guidelines for Libraries and Archives in New York State* (Albany, NY: New York State Library, 1991) provides a detailed description and design components of a good heating, ventilating, and air-conditioning (HVAC) system.

Photographs

Photographic materials have many special requirements for their preservation, processing, appraisal, and administration. A good work to begin studying their special properties is Mary Lynn Ritzenthaler's manual *Archives and Manuscripts: Administration of Photographic Collections* (Chicago: Society of American Archivists, 1984).

Another good work devoted to 19th-century photographs is James M. Reilly, *Care and*

Identification of 19th Century Photographic Prints (Rochester, NY: Eastman Kodak Co., 1986).

Film

Information on the proper care for film archives is also difficult to find. The recently published work, *A Handbook for Film Archives Two,* edited by Eileen Bowser and John Kuiper (New York: Garland Publishing, 1991) should make reliable information a little more accessible. An older work in this area is Paul L. Gordon's *The Book of Film Care,* Kodak Publication H-23 (Rochester, NY: Eastman Kodak Co., 1983), although archivist should still turn to the Bowser and Kuiper work for the most recent preservation developments regarding film care. For a bibliography of books and articles dealing with a variety of media, see Mary B. Bowling, "Literature on the Preservation of Nonpaper Materials," *American Archivist* 53 (Spring 1990), pp. 340-348.

Oral History

Oral history has come to play a vital role in helping to document groups that do not leave a written legacy or in enhancing the written legacy. Frederick J. Steilow's award-winning publication, *The Management of Oral History Sound Archives* (Westport, CT: Greenwood Press, 1986) is the most current and broadest treatment of the oral history process. An interesting article on the importance and possibilities is James E. Fogerty, "Filling the Gap : Oral History in the Archives," *American Archivist* 46 (Spring 1983) pp. 148-157.

Two classic works on the mechanics of developing, implementing, and carrying out a good oral history program are Willa K. Baum's books *Oral History for the Local Historical Society* (Nashville, TN: American Association for State and Local History, 1971) and *Transcribing and Editing Oral History* (Nashville, TN: American Association for State and Local History, 1977).

Sound Recordings

An important and related issue to producing oral histories is the preservation of all types of recorded media. Christopher Ann Paton has written two recent articles concerning this subject which present up-to-date information. The first is "Whispers in the Stacks: The Problem of Sound Recordings in Archives," *American Archivist* 53 (Spring 1990), pp. 274-280; it is a starting point for archivists who have any type of recorded sound in their stacks. The second is the "Annotated Selected Bibliography of Works Relating to Sound Recordings and Magnetic and Optical Media," *Midwestern Archivist* 16, no. 1 (1991), pp. 31-47. This issue of the *Midwestern Archivist* is dedicated to articles on the management and preservation of sound archives in a variety of formats.

Alan Ward's *A Manual of Sound Archive Administration* (Brookfield, VT: Gower Publishing Company, 1990) is a recent book dealing with the problems associated with recorded sound materials. The Ward book was originally published in England, so some sections (e.g., copyright) are less applicable in the United States. This book is readily available in the United States through the Society of American Archivists.

Micrographics

The prize-winning work by Nancy Gwinn, *Preservation Microfilming: A Guide for Librarians and Archivists* (Chicago: American Library Association, 1987) is an excellent starting point for institutions interested in establishing a preservation microfilming program.

The RLG Preservation Microfilming Handbook, Nancy E. Elkington, ed., (Mountainview, CA: Research Libraries Group, 1992) is a comprehensive guide to preservation microfilming. The handbook features both theoretical and practical discussions of topics including guidelines for preservation microfilming projects, technical standards, and implementation issues. It contains the most up-to-date technical standards information.

Electronic Records

A place to begin a study of electronic records is the National Archives and Records Administration's June 1991 bibliography "Management of Electronic Records," compiled by Jeffery T. Hartley.

Theory and practice concerning the management of electronic records is rapidly becoming important to all archivists. Important works to study are Charles M. Dollar, *Archival Theory and Information Technologies: The Impact of Information Technologies on Archival Principles and Methods* (Macerata, Italy: University of Macerata, 1992), number 1 of the Informatics and Documentation Series, Otto Bucci, ed.; David Bearman, ed., *Archives and Museum Informatics Technical Report No. 13* (Pittsburgh: Archives and Museum Informatics, 1991); and Katherine Gavrel, *Conceptual Problems Posed by Electronic Records: A RAMP Study* (Paris, France: UNESCO, International Council on Archives, 1990).

Digital Imaging

Digital imaging is now seen as a tool for both archival preservation and access. Three project reports describe the process, as well as the issues involved: Gerald Stone and Philip Sylvaim, "Archivista: A New Horizon in Providing Access to Visual Records of the National Archives of Canada," Archivaria 33 (Winter 1991-92), pp. 253-265; Anne R. Kenney, *Preserving Archival Material through Digital Technology: A Cooperative Demonstration Project* (Ithaca, NY: Cornell University Press, 1993). See also National Archives and Records Administration, Archival Research and Evaluation Staff, *Optical Digital Image Storage Systems: Project Report* (Washington, DC: U.S. Government Printing Office, 1991). Appendix A of this report provides a good introductory overview to digital imaging.

Maps and Architectural Drawings

A good introduction into the collection, appraisal, organization, and preservation of maps and architectural drawings is Ralph E. Ehrenberg, *Archives and Manuscripts: Maps and Architectural Drawings* (Chicago: Society of American Archivists, 1982). Nancy Carlson Schrock and Mary Campbell Cooper, eds., Records in Architectural Offices: Suggestions for *the Organization, Storage, and Conservation of Architectural Office Records* , 3rd ed. (Boston, MA: COPAR, 1992) describes the problems of dealing with architectural records in a working office.

Archival Directories

One means of locating other archival programs in a given region is through the *Directory of Archives and Manuscript Repositories in the United States*, 2nd ed. (Phoenix, AZ: Oryx Press, 1988, 2nd. ed.). This guide provides a list of institutional archives, manuscript repositories, historical societies, etc. in the United States and provides descriptions of their holdings. The *National Union Catalog of Manuscript Collections* also lists respoitories that report holdings to the Library of Congress. This latter work covers primarily manuscript repositories, not institutional archives.

The two national online bibliographic networks mentioned in this book—the Research Libraries Information Network (RLIN) and the Online Computer Library Center (OCLC)—also list archival materials in a variety of repositories.

Archival and Related Associations

National Archival Organizations

Society of American Archivists (SAA)
600 South Federal, Suite 504
Chicago, IL 60605
(312) 922-0140
Publications: *American Archivist; Archival Outlook*

National Association of Government
   Archives and Records Administrators
   (NAGARA)
Executive Secretariat
New York State Archives and
   Records Administration
10A46 Cultural Education Center
Albany, NY 12230
(518) 473-8037
Publication: *Clearinghouse*

American Association for State and Local
   History (AASLH)
172 Second Avenue North, Suite 102
Nashville, TN 37201
(615) 255-2971
Publications: *History News; History News Dispatch*

Association of Records Managers and
   Administrators (ARMA)
4200 Somerset Drive, Suite 215
Prairie Village, KA 66208
(913) 341-3808
Publication: *Records Management Quarterly*

Association of Canadian Archivists (ACA)
P. O. Box 2596-Station D
Ottawa, Ontario
Canada K1P 5W6
(613) 443-0251
Publication: *Archivaria*

American Library Association (ALA)
50 East Huron Street
Chicago, IL 60611
1-800-545-2433
Publication: *American Libraries*

Association of Catholic Diocesan Archivists
    (ACDA)
Sr. Catherine Louise LaCoste, Secretary
Diocese of San Diego - Archives
P. O. Box 85728
San Diego, CA 92186-5728
(619) 297-8190
Publication: *ACDA Bulletin*

Association of Moving Image Archivists
    (AMIA)
Office of the AMIA Secretariat
c/o National Center for Film and Video
    Preservation
The American Film Institute
2021 North Western Avenue
Los Angeles, CA 90027
(213) 856-7637
Publication: *AMIA Newsletter*

Association for Recorded Sound Collections
(ARSC)
Executive Director
P. O. Box 10162
Silver Spring, MD 20914

Regional and Local Archival Organizations

Every region of the United States has an archival association. Also, many states and metropolitan areas also have a formal or informal archival group. To locate the archival organization nearest you, contact the Society of American Archivists headquarters in Chicago, Illinois.

Preservation and Conservation Organizations

Northeast Document Conservation Center
    (NEDCC)
100 Brickstone Street
Andover, MA 01810-1428
(508) 470-1010

Conservation Center for Art and Historic
    Artifacts
264 South 23rd Street
Philadelphia, PA 19103
(215) 545-0613

American Institute for the Conservation of
    Historic and Artistic Works (AIC)
1400 16th Street, NW, Suite 340
Washington, D.C. 20036
(202) 232-6636

Appendix A—Model Deed of Gift for Donation of Historical Materials

Model Deed of Gift for Donation of Historical Materials

This deed of gift has been designed as a model that may be used in whole or in part, as appropriate, for donations of historical materials to an archives. Alternative paragraphs that could be substituted at the donor's request for paragraphs in the body of the model deed are placed together at its conclusion.

Gift of Papers and Other Historical Materials

of

_____

to the

_____ Archives

1. Subject to the terms and conditions hereinafter set forth, I, _____
_____ (hereinafter referred to as the Donor), hereby give, donate, and convey to _____ (hereinafter referred to as the Donee) for deposit in the _____ Archives, my papers and other historical materials (hereinafter referred to as the Materials) which are described in Appendix A, attached hereto.

2. Title to the Materials shall pass to the Donee upon their delivery to the Donee.

3. Following delivery, the Materials shall be maintained by the Donee in the _____ Archives. At any time after delivery and subject to the provisions of paragraph 5, the Donor shall be permitted freely to examine any of the Materials during the regular working hours of the _____ Archives.

4. It is the Donor's wish that the Materials be made available for research as soon as possible, consistent with the General Restriction Policy of the _____ Archives, following their deposit in the _____ Archives. The Donee shall have the Materials reviewed and shall restrict access to those Materials the use of which should be restricted in accordance with the normal application of the General Restriction Policy of the _____ Archives.

5. Following the completion of the review provided for above, materials so restricted shall not be made available for inspection, reading, or use by anyone, except regular employees of the Donee in the performance of normal archival work on such Materials, and the Donor, or persons authorized by him in writing to have access to such materials.

6. Notwithstanding the provisions of paragraph 5, Materials covered by this instrument shall be subject to subpoena or other lawful process, subject further to any rights, privileges or defenses that the Donor, the Donee or any other person may invoke to prevent compliance with said subpoena or other lawful process. To insure Donor the opportunity to raise such rights, privileges, or defenses, the Donee shall notify the Donor or his representative, so long as the Donor lives, as expeditiously as possible of the receipt of such subpoena or other lawful process.

7.   Materials which have been restricted from access as herein provided shall be reviewed by the Donee from time to time and any Materials which, because of the passage of time or other circumstances, no longer require such restrictions shall be opened to public access.

8.   Subject to the restrictions imposed herein, the Donee may dispose of any of the Materials which the Donee determines are not required by the _____ Archives.

9.   The Donor hereby gives and assigns to the Donee all rights of copyright which the Donor has in (a) the Materials and (b) in such of his works as may be found among any collections of Materials received by the Donee from others.

10.   In the event that the Donor may from time to time hereafter give, donate, and convey to the Donee, for deposit in the _____ Archives, additional papers and other historical Materials, title to such additional papers and other historical Materials shall pass to the Donee upon their delivery, and all of the provisions of this instrument of gift shall be applicable to such additional papers and other historical Materials. A description of the additonal papers and other historical Materials so donated and delivered shall be prepared and attached hereto.

Signed: _____
                                    Donor

Date: _____

The foregoing gift of the papers and other historical Materials of the Donor is accepted on behalf of the _____ Archives, subject to the terms and conditions heretofore set forth.

Signed: _____
                                    Donee

Date: _____

Appendix A

Attached to and forming part of the instrument of gift of papers and other historical Materials, executed by _____ (Depositor) on _____ (*date*) and accepted by the _____ (Archives) on _____ (*date*).

Appendix B, C, etc.

The following additional papers and other historical Materials are donated to and accepted by the _____ Archives pursuant to the instrument of gift executed by _____ (Depositor) on _____ (*date*) and accepted by the _____ (Archives) on _____ (*date*).

Appendix B—Outline of a Model Procedures Manual

Overview of processing:
    Principles of arrangement and description
    Administration and staff responsibilities
    Physical facilities and rules for handling records
Accessioning:
    Boxing and listing on site
    Physical transfer procedures and forms
    Accessioning forms
    Acknowledgement procedures
    Separation of nontextual records
        photographs
        films
        sound recordings
        videotapes
        computer tapes and disks
        maps and architectural materials
        posters and broadsides
        publications
    Identifying separate collections within an accession
    Reboxing and labeling
    Recording basic information and checking for related collections
    Preparing container lists
Arrangement:
    Reviewing collection file and surveying collection
    Preparation and approval of work plan
    Basic research on records and creators
    Intellectual organization by creators and file sets
    Physical organization by file sets and boxes
    Deciding when to retain/discard original order
    Imposing an arrangement—choosing a system
    Folder-level organization and folder labeling
    Item-level organization
    Weeding duplicates and identifying routine records for appraisal
    Identifying restricted records
    Identifying records with potential confidentiality problems
    Labeling boxes and folders
Preservation during processing:
    Boxing records
    Refoldering
    Photocopying
    Flattening
    Removing fasteners
    Cleaning
    Identifying problems for Conservation Department
Description:
    Internal finding aids—nature and structure
    Deciding on level of detail and type of finding aids
    Staff responsibilities
    Describing records creators

Description (continued):
   Describing records
   Describing archival activities
   Final container listings
   Entering information into repository catalogs and indexes
   Preparing the descriptive information—
      finding standard forms of names and places
      finding standard subject index terms
      applying standard forms and terms
   Style
      punctuation
      spelling
      spacing
      abbreviations
   Filing rules
   Editing descriptions
   Preparing summary descriptions for:
      institutional publications (narrative descriptions)
      bibliographic utility (MARC entry or entries)
Administrative requirements:
   Reporting procedures
   Keeping track of supplies, time, and facilities used
   Updating information as processing proceeds
Appendices:
   Forms—blank and samples
   Processing checklist
   Sources of information for terms
   Technical cataloging manuals
   Structure of USMARC format and applicable AACR2 rules

Appendix C—Sample User Registration Forms

Colorado's Campus in the Sky

FORT LEWIS COLLEGE

CENTER OF SOUTHWEST STUDIES
1000 RIM DR., DURANGO, CO 81301   TELEPHONE 303/247-7456

USER REGISTRATION FORM

The Center's archives and special collections are open without fee to students, faculty and staff of the College, and members of the public, for non-circulating use only. Access to certain collections may be restricted, as explained in the Center's general restriction policy statement. Your registration on this form will help us to protect the historical materials and will enable us to evaluate the usefulness of the Center's holdings.

DATE _____ / _____ / _____
Month   Day   Year

NAME _____
Surname   First   Middle

PHONE _____

HOME ADDRESS _____
Street/ P.O. Box   City   State   Zip Code

LOCAL ADDRESS _____
(if different from above)   Street/ P.O. Box   City   Local Phone Number

PHOTO ID _____ ( ) ( ) (_____) _____ / _____
Number   FLC   Driver's License   Other; specify   Expir. Date

Would you like your name to be on our mailing list? ( ) ( ) {Please initial}
yes   no

USER DESCRIPTION:
( ) FLC Faculty--Department_____
( ) FLC Staff--Office/Dept._____
( ) FLC Student--Major_____
( ) Other Academic Institution_____ ( ) ( ) ( )
( ) General Public_____   Faculty Staff Student

NATURE OF RESEARCH:
( ) Research Paper_____
        Proposed Topic   Department   Course Number

( ) Publication_____
        Proposed Topic   Name of Publication

( ) Administrative_____
        Subject   Office or Department

( ) Other (Please specify)_____
        Subject

May we inform another user studying a similar topic that you are researching this topic? ( ) ( )
yes   no

GUIDELINES FOR USING THE MATERIALS ("the records") AT THE CENTER:

1. All users must register (this form), showing positive current photo identification and signing the user log daily.
2. Due to preservation concerns, food, drink, and smoking are not permitted in the research area.
3. Keep the records in their present arrangement; loose pages will stay in order if turned like pages in a book.
4. Please only use one folder of materials at a time.
5. To preserve the originals for future use, please make no marks or erasures or other changes in the records.
6. Due to the risk of inadvertent damage to documents, use of ink is prohibited; please take notes in pencil.
7. Photocopying is permitted, if it is in accordance with donor agreements and copyright restrictions, unless the item is fragile, exceptionally valuable, or too large. When allowed, it is limited to single copies for the user's reference use only. Ask research room attendant for assistance.
8. These materials are provided for reference use only. The user agrees to publish no portion of them without the written permission of the Center, and assumes sole responsibility for any infringement of the literary rights, copyrights, or other rights which pertain to these materials.
9. With the exception of some books, the records may not circulate; they must stay at the Center.
10. Theft, destruction or mutilation of the materials is a crime (Colorado Revised Statutes §24-90-117).
11. The user agrees to give the Center a complimentary copy of any publication relying heavily on its collections.
12. Citations should follow this format: identification of item, name of collection, Center of Southwest Studies, Fort Lewis College.
13. The user must read and sign this form before using the records. By signing this form, the user acknowledges responsibility to observe the above guidelines.
14. The Center of Southwest Studies wishes to provide its collections for use in every way consistent with good scholarship, productive research, and archival preservation. Your comments and suggestions are welcome.

*Signature of User*_____   *Date*_____

{THIS SIDE IS FOR STAFF USE ONLY}

User #_____   Personal visit (   )   Letter (   )   Telephone (   )
Date(s) other side updated:_____

SOURCES USED:

Shelf Location	Collection/Record Group	Items	Staff	Date

DOCUMENTS COPIED:

Shelf Location	Collection/Record Group	Items	Staff	Date

PHOTOGRAPHS COPIED:

Shelf Location	Collection/Record Group	Items	Staff	Date

Appendix D—Sample Photoduplication Request Form

CENTER OF SOUTHWEST STUDIES

1000 RIM DRIVE, DURANGO, CO 81301-3999   TELEPHONE 303/247-7456

PHOTODUPLICATION REQUEST FORM

The Center's historical materials--other than those covered by our General Restriction Policy Statement and any specific restrictions--are accessible to the public. Copies of these materials may be made, unless restricted by federal copyright law and any collection-specific stipulations, for a charge that enables the Center to offer this service.

NAME_____   PHONE #_____
        Surname   First   Middle

ADDRESS_____
        Street/ P.O. Box   City   State   Zip Code
INSTITUTIONAL AFFILIATION_____

NOTICE
WARNING CONCERNING COPYRIGHT RESTRICTIONS

The copyright law of the United States (Title 17, United States Code) governs the making of photocopies or other reproductions of copyrighted material.

Under certain conditions specified in the law, libraries and archives are authorized to furnish a photocopy or other reproduction. One of these specified conditions is that the photocopy or reproduction is not to be "used for any purpose other than private study, scholarship, or research." If a user makes a request for, or later uses, a photocopy or reproduction for purposes in excess of "fair use," that user may be liable for copyright infringement.

This institution reserves the right to refuse to accept a copying order if, in its judgment, fulfillment of the order would involve violation of copyright law.

In compliance with the copyright law, the Center of Southwest Studies limits the number of copies of each item to <u>one</u>. Furthermore, we cannot copy all or substantially all of a work for you unless an unused copy of the work cannot be found at a fair price. In addition, we reserve the right to restrict the use or reproduction of rare, valuable, or fragile items; to ensure that the use of the reproductions is in good taste; and to make special quotations on items involving unusual difficulty in copying; and to charge a use fee for staff time in excess of one half hour to fulfill this reproduction request.

PHOTODUPLICATION REQUEST

I request reproduction of the following material(s). The following is each item's identifying number, collection title, and brief description. *(Continue on back of this form if necessary.)*

Purpose(s) for which the copied material is to be used:

I agree to use the copied material(s) **only for my private study, scholarship, or research.** I understand that it is my responsibility to abide by copyright laws, including obtaining permission from the copyright owner for any other use of the copied material(s). I will not duplicate the copied material without securing the permission of the copyright owner. Furthermore, I agree to credit the Center and the collection in any work drawn from my use of the Center's historical materials and to provide the Center a complimentary copy of any publication or production substantially based on the Center's materials.

Special instructions for reproduction:

*Signature of User*_____   *Date*_____
                    {BELOW IS FOR STAFF USE ONLY}
REPRODUCTION COST: $_____.____   ORDER WILL BE READY BY_____
HANDLING/MAILING FEE:$_____.____   SW CENTER USER #_____
USE FEE: $_____.____   PAYABLE TO **Center of Southwest Studies**
TOTAL PAYMENT DUE: $_____.____ $ RECEIVED BY (staff initials)_____
AMOUNT PAID: $_____.____   DATE PAID:_____/_____/_____

                                                    SW-18   October 4, 1993

CENTER OF SOUTHWEST STUDIES
1000 RIM DRIVE, DURANGO, CO 81301-3999   TELEPHONE 303/247-7456

PHOTOGRAPH DUPLICATION REQUEST FORM

The Center's historical images--other than those covered by our General Restriction Policy Statement and any specific restrictions--are accessible to the public. Copies of photographs are available, unless restricted by federal copyright law and/or any collection-specific stipulations, for a charge that is based on the size of the photo, whether or not the Center already has a negative, and based on the purchaser's intended use of the image. With completion of this form and payment of all appropriate fees, the Center grants permission to use the photographs listed in the manner described.

CONDITIONS OF USE
In consideration of our supplying you with a copy of a photograph, the user agrees:
1. to use the image **only once** and then only for the purpose stated on this form, and
2. to pay for the cost of producing a negative (which the Center retains) if the Center does not have a negative for a photograph requested, and
3. to credit each individual reproduction to: Fort Lewis College Center of Southwest Studies, and
4. to make advance payment to the Center of reproduction and use fees, and
5. not to use or authorize others to use the image for any purpose differing from the specific use stated below without written permission from the Center of Southwest Studies, and
6. to provide the Center, at the Center's request, a complimentary copy of any publication or production using a Center photograph.

The Center of Southwest Studies reserves the right to limit the number of photographic copies: to restrict the use or reproduction of rare, valuable, or fragile items; to ensure that the use of the reproductions is in good taste; to make special quotations on items involving unusual difficulty in copying; and to charge a higher cost than specified for reproduction of a small number of special items. The Center reserves the right to require a proof for approval before publication.

USE FEE SCHEDULE   These fees are in addition to reproduction, handling, and mailing fees.
(Please check the appropriate line)

Non-commercial Use
____ 1. For personal research or display in a private home .... no fee
____ 2. Fee per image for use by non-profit organizations, by the media in newspaper or magazine articles, newscasts or non-commercial documentaries, and for non-commercial publication by university presses. *Describe:*_____ $ 1.00

Commercial Use
1. Fee per image for use in a book, filmstrip, videotape, poster, postcard, calendar, or similar commercial use, **per edition.** *Describe:*_____
____ a. 1 to 5,000 copies $10.00
____ b. 5,001 to 10,000 copies 30.00
____ c. 10,001 to 25,000 copies 75.00
____ d. over 25,000 copies 100.00
2. Fee per image for use in published serial. *Serial title/date:*_____
____ a. circulation under 50,000 .... $10.00
____ b. circulation 50,001 to 100,000 .... 30.00
____ c. circulation over 100,000 .... 100.00
3. Special use fees, per image. *Describe:*_____
____ a. for commercial decorative display (offices, public areas, etc.)............................. $25.00
____ b. for use on a book jacket by a commercial publisher 50.00
____ c. for use on commercial motion picture or television 75.00
____ d. for advertising 100.00
If ten or more photograph are used in a single display, publication, or production, a flat fee will be negotiated. Requests for copies of graphic items intended for single mass reproductions such as posters, postcards, or note paper may be subject to special contractual procedures.

Non-Profit or Academic Use (for non-profit corporations and scholars publishing instructional media)
____ Use fee per image for filmstrips, videotapes, posters, or similar use...................................... $ 1.00
If five or more images are used in a single production, a flat fee will be negotiated.

Special Consideration
The Center of Southwest Studies reserves the right to waive the above use fees or other requirements on an individual basis. Such waiver can be made only upon written application.

NAME_____ **PHONE #**_____
                 Surname   First   Middle

ADDRESS_____
                 Street/ P.O. Box   City   State   Zip Code

INSTITUTIONAL AFFILIATION_____

NOTICE
WARNING CONCERNING COPYRIGHT RESTRICTIONS

The copyright law of the United States (Title 17, United States Code) governs the making of photocopies or other reproductions of copyrighted material.

Under certain conditions specified in the law, libraries and archives are authorized to furnish a photocopy or other reproduction. One of these specified conditions is that the photocopy or reproduction is not to be "used for any purpose other than private study, scholarship, or research." If a user makes a request for, or later uses, a photocopy or reproduction for purposes in excess of "fair use," that user may be liable for copyright infringement.

This institution reserves the right to refuse to accept a copying order if, in its judgment, fulfillment of the order would involve violation of copyright law.

PHOTOREPRODUCTION REQUEST

I request reproduction of the following photograph(s). I have noted each item's identifying number and/or brief description. *(Continue on an attached page if necessary.)*
All prints will have a glossy finish unless a matte finish is specified.

Photograph description	**Size**	**Finish**	**Neg. #**

I agree to use the copy photograph(s) **only once** and then only for the following stated purpose:

Special instructions to photo lab:

Purchase of photographs constitutes agreement to comply with the conditions of use stated on this form. Handling fee is $3 per photo.

*Signature of User*_____   *Date*_____

{BELOW IS FOR STAFF USE ONLY}

REPRODUCTION COST:	$_____.____	ORDER WILL BE READY BY_____
NEGATIVE FEE:	$_____.____	SW CENTER USER #_____
USE FEE(S):	$_____.____	PAYABLE TO **Center of Southwest Studies**
HANDLING/MAILING FEE:	$_____.____	DATE PAID: _____/____/____
TOTAL PAYMENT DUE:	$_____.____	AMOUNT PAID: $_____.____

SW-04   October 4, 1993

Appendix F—Sample Loan Agreement

LOAN AGREEMENT
BETWEEN
THE MARYKNOLL MISSION ARCHIVES
AND

NAME _____

INSTITUTION _____

ADDRESS _____

CITY _____ STATE _____ ZIP CODE _____

PERSON RESPONSIBLE FOR BORROWED ITEM(S) _____

TELEPHONE NUMBER _____

PURPOSE OF LOAN _____

LOCATION OF EXHIBITION _____

TITLE OF EXHIBITION _____

DATES OF EXHIBITION: (FROM) _____ (TO) _____

ITEMS WILL BE RETURNED NO LATER THAN _____
    (If items are retained longer than stated, all other permissions, including
    copyright and use permissions are revoked immediately.)

DESCRIPTION OF ITEMS BORROWED:

APPROXIMATE VALUE OF OBJECTS BORROWED _____

INSURANCE WILL BE CARRIED BY _____

I, _____, have read the rules and regulations regarding items on loan
from the Maryknoll Mission Archives on the reverse side of this form. I agree to the above
conditions of loan and I am authorized to agree thereto:

For the _____

Signature _____

TITLE _____

Date _____

For the MARYKNOLL MISSION
ARCHIVES

Signature _____

TITLE _____

Date _____

**CONDITIONS, RULES, AND REGULATIONS FOR ITEMS ON LOAN FROM THE
MARYKNOLL MISSION ARCHIVES**

1. Each item, including documentary material, must be labelled and credited in any brochure
or other publication as from the MARYKNOLL MISSION ARCHIVES. Unless otherwise agreed
to in writing, no reproductions are permitted except photographic copies for catalog and
publicity uses related to the stated purpose of this loan.

2. Each item, including documentary material, is loaned for the benefit of the borrower and
shall be given special care at all times to insure against loss, damage, or deterioration.

3. All loaned materials should be properly handled at all times and should not be exposed to
undue levels of light, heat, or other deleterious elements. If the items are loaned for
exhibition, the MARYKNOLL MISSION ARCHIVES asks that the exhibit area not be
permanently lighted and that filters be applied to any ultraviolet lights in the exhibition area.

4. Documents and objects shall be insured during this loan period by the borrower.

5. The borrower shall indemnify the CATHOLIC FOREIGN MISSION SOCIETY OF AMERICA,
INC. and/or the MARYKNOLL SISTERS OF ST. DOMINIC, INC. against all claims, actions,
proceedings, costs, damages, and liabilities, including attorney's fees, arising out of,
connected with, or resulting from the use of, or the borrowing of, the objects.

6. All costs of shipping, packing, transportation, and insurance will be assumed by the
borrower.

7. Objects must be returned to the MARYKNOLL MISSION ARCHIVES by the date agreed
upon on the reverse side of this agreement.

8. In the event of any conflict between this agreement and any standard policy forms of the
borrower, the terms of this agreement shall be controlling. No modification of this agreement
shall be effective unless it is in writing.

9. Without permission of the MARYKNOLL MISSION ARCHIVES, the borrower shall not (a)
assign, transfer, pledge, or hypothecate this agreement, the objects or any part thereof or any
interest therein; (b) sublet or lend the objects or any part thereof; (c) permit the objects or any
part thereof to be used by anyone other than the borrower; or (d) permit the objects to be
removed from the location specified upon the face of this agreement. The objects shall be
used only for the purposes specified upon the face of this agreement. The property is and
shall at all times remain the property of the Catholic Foreign Mission Society of America, Inc.
and/or the Maryknoll Sisters of St. Dominic, Inc. and the borrower shall have no right, title,
or interest therein except as expressly set forth in this agreement.

Notes

1. All definitions in this manual are derived from Lynn Lady Bellardo and Lewis Bellardo, eds., *The Glossary of Archivists, Manuscript Curators, and Records Managers* (Chicago: Society of American Archivists, 1992).
2. *A Donor's Guide* (Chicago: Society of American Archivists, 1980).
3. James M. O'Toole, *Understanding Archives and Manuscripts* (Chicago: Society of American Archivists, 1990).
4. Thomas Wilsted and William Nolte, *Managing Archival and Manuscript Repositories* (Chicago: Society of American Archivists, 1991), p. 29.
5. Paul McCarthy, *Archives Assessment and Planning Workbook* (Chicago: Society of American Archivists, 1989).
6. *Strengthening New York's Historical Records Programs: A Self Study Guide* (Albany, NY: State Archives and Records Administration, 1988).
7. *Guide and Resources for Archival Strategic Planning (GRASP)* (Atlanta: National Association of Government Archives and Records Administration, 1990).
8. F. Gerald Ham, *Selecting and Appraising Archives and Manuscripts* (Chicago: Society of American Archivists, 1992).
9. *The Code of Ethics for Archivists* (Chicago: Society of American Archivists, 1992).
10. Fredric M. Miller, *Arranging and Describing Archives and Manuscripts* (Chicago: Society of American Archivists, 1990).
11. Oliver Wendell Holmes, "Archival Arrangement—Five Different Operations at Five Different Levels," *American Archivist* 27 (January 1964): 21-41.
12. Mary Jo Pugh, *Providing Reference Services for Archives and Manuscripts* (Chicago: Society of American Archivists, 1992).

13. Karen Motylewski, "What an Institution Can Do to Survey Its Own Preservation Needs," Technical Leaflet (Andover, MA: Northeast Document Conservation Center, 1991).

14. Mary Lynn Ritzenthaler, *Preserving Archives and Manuscripts* (Chicago: Society of American Archivists, 1993).

15. For detailed specifications of an HVAC system, see William P. Lull, *Conservation Environment Guidelines for Libraries and Archives in New York State* (Albany, NY: New York State Library, 1991).

16. Charles M. Dollar, *Archival Theory and Information Technologies: The Impact of Information Technologies on Archival Principles and Methods* (Macerata, Italy: University of Macerata, 1992).

17. Peter Adelstein, "The Latest Word on 'Archival'," *SAA Newsletter*, November 1991: 14-15.

18. Nancy Gwinn, *Preservation Microfilming: A Guide for Librarians and Archivists* (Chicago: American Library Association, 1987).

19. NAGARA/NARA, "Optical Media Systems: Management Issues," Joint Report, NARA and NAGARA, 1991.

Index